THE JOY CART

The True Story of a Boy and His Toys

by Marvin Bartlett

Independence Books
Baltimore

Second printing

ISBN: 1-58851-144-8
PUBLISHED BY INDEPENDENCE BOOKS
www.independencebooks.com
Baltimore

Printed in the United States of America

Acknowledgments

This book is the result of a lot of encouragement from many people. First, I'd like to thank Doug and Jennifer Mynear for their openness and patience with me as I conducted more than a hundred hours of interviews with them and their friends. It can't be easy to recount so many painful memories and be so honest about your emotions, yet they were always gracious.

Thanks to John Lynch, the editor of Lexington Family Magazine, for giving me story-telling advice, and to literary agent K.J. Vigue II for lighting a fire under me to write a book in the first place. The cover design and some of the photos are courtesy of my good and talented friends, John Lackey and Don Barker. The cover portrait is used by permission of the University of Kentucky Children's Hospital. Some information for Chapter 29 comes with permission from "My Story About Cancer," by Charles B. Wolford (Seven Locks Press, 1999).

Above all, I have to thank Jarrett. It's impossible to have a negative attitude about anything when you're around him. His story should help us all appreciate the millions of unheralded examples of courage and faith exhibited by cancer survivors, including the 12,400 children who are diagnosed each year. My own mother inspires those around her with the same upbeat outlook on life as she continues to triumph over bone cancer. May we all recognize the angels among us.

Thank you, Jarrett, for showing us that it truly is more blessed to give than to receive.

==========

By purchasing this book, you have made a donation to ensure that Jarrett's Joy Cart continues to operate for years to come.

Foreword

When Marvin first asked me if he could write a book about The Joy Cart and me, I thought it was pretty crazy. I couldn't see why anyone would want to read about a kid who's battled cancer most of his life. That doesn't make for very fun reading. But then I thought of all the things I've learned and done because of my cancer.

I decided to let Marvin write this book because I want other people facing tough situations to know that you can get through most anything if you keep a positive attitude and remember helping others is the best way to help yourself.

There aren't enough words to tell my family, friends, the medical staff and the Jarrett's Joy Cart volunteers and supporters how much I appreciate all they've done. This story would be very different if it weren't for all of you.

~JARRETT MYNEAR
February 2002

1
The Videotape

It was crunch time in the television newsroom–that time of day when you're really up against the deadline. It's the hour when almost every reporter is back from the field, scrambling to type last-second information into their scripts, get videotape edited and phone calls returned. It's a crazy, hectic atmosphere that true journalists love and outside observers find disturbing.

As I made my way through the mayhem to my desk, I wondered if anyone would notice my eyes were watery. Surely, as big as it felt, that lump in my throat would be visible. I had just viewed a few minutes of videotape of a little boy who was fighting some kind of cancer and it affected me.

The tape had been shot earlier in the day by a videographer who was sent to the University of Kentucky Children's Hospital by himself. The planned news conference wasn't deemed important enough to require a reporter. It was basketball season in Kentucky, "March Madness," a time when the UK Wildcats were expected to bulldoze their way through all competition and make it to the Final Four. It seemed half our staff was on the road with the team and the other half was scraping up local sidebar stories. If you own a business with "Wildcat" in the name, it may get you a shot on the nightly news in March. If you skip work to watch an afternoon basketball game at a local bar (and thousands do), you may have a camera stuck in your face. The mayor of Lexington declares every day UK is playing a tournament game as "Blue-White Day," meaning you could be chastised by friends and neighbors if you forgot to put on the team colors before you headed out of the house that morning. It's said that basketball is a religion in Kentucky. Our newscasts can sometimes look like a worship service.

That's why the shooter had been instructed to "spray" the news conference. In newsroom lingo, that means "get in and out quickly." We wouldn't have much room for the story in the basketball-heavy show that night.

Little did any of us know that the boy who was the focus of the news conference that day would soon touch us all so deeply.

My assignment, as a reporter/anchor, was to view the tape, pick a short sound bite and write a 40-second story for the 5 p.m. newscast. That was my introduction to Jarrett Mynear.

What I saw was a small boy, nine years old at the time, who was more articulate than any child I had ever seen interviewed. Usually when we try to interview someone that age, we get yes and no answers, a whole lot of shoulder shrugs and we hear "I don't know" over and over again. That's OK. They're little kids. They're not expected to wax poetic.

Yet here was Jarrett, speaking in complete and thought-provoking sentences. He had one of those "Owen Meany" type voices. Fans of John Irving will know immediately what I mean. He spoke with a squeak, a sound that commands your attention because of its uniqueness.

The news conference revealed that a new sight would soon be seen around the children's ward. "Jarrett's Joy Cart" would deliver free toys twice a month to every child who was a patient there. And here's where he got me. Jarrett, sitting at a table with his head barely peeking above the microphones, said he knew what it was like to spend most of your life in a hospital.

"Kids get bored and depressed in here," he said. "Some of them never get any visitors."

He said he wanted to deliver toys on a regular schedule to give the patients something to look forward to.

He said it with such sincerity that I knew it wasn't rehearsed. It was the squeaky voice of experience, from someone who should be out on the playground or tossing pebbles in a creek–not someone who should have any idea what it means to spend weeks hooked up to intravenous tubes, facing surgery upon surgery.

As if the words weren't enough to make a direct hit on my soft spot, the pictures sealed the deal. Jarrett had a large bald spot on the back of his head, a circle that marked the spot of one surgery. I later learned that he liked to compare himself to Friar Tuck and that does indeed best describe his appearance at the time.

After the news conference, the videographer followed The Joy Cart on its inaugural run from room to room and another surprise showed up on the tape. The boy limped. His right leg was artificial.

With the lump forming in my throat as I viewed the tape, comic relief came at just the right time. As Jarrett pushed the hospital cart loaded with stuffed animals, games and puzzles, it got away from him and banged into a wall. Clearly, the microphone picked up his response: "I'm not a very good driver today. I've had too much Coke to drink."

Normally, when writing such a short story about a news conference, I wouldn't even watch the whole tape. But I watched everything we had recorded at the hospital that day and knew right away we had to do more. We weren't doing this story justice. But I banged out the copy for the short segment on the computer, edited the tape and put it in the mix of things that were about to air.

I watched on a monitor in the newsroom as the story was broadcast live and checked out the reactions of the others around me. These "hardened" journalists who had seen their share of crime, corruption and coroner's cases were touched too, just as I had been. Jarrett had captured everyone's attention in a ten-second sound bite.

I heard my colleagues utter phrases that would probably embarrass most nine-year-old boys.

"He's precious."

"What an angel!"

"How cute!"

The descriptions fit. As we would all soon learn, The Joy Cart was destined to do more than deliver toys. It would become a symbol of hope and inspiration to cancer patients everywhere. And the boy behind it, full of Coke or not, would become the best example imaginable of someone who turned life's lemons into lemonade.

7

2
Baby Talk

Doug Mynear had hoped to have a date when he managed to get two tickets to the University of Kentucky basketball game that January night in 1983. It should've been easy bait. UK tickets are as precious as jewels in Central Kentucky and more difficult to come by. And the opponent was Southeastern Conference rival Louisiana State University. UK fans loved to come out to heckle Dale Brown, LSU's colorful coach.

But as fate would have it, Doug's date backed out and he had to take his roommate to the game. It turned out to be a wonderful change in plans.

Before the game, a crowd milled around in the Lexington Civic Center just outside Rupp Arena, one of the great shrines of basketball. As Doug and his roommate Mike rode the escalator down to the center's first floor food court, Mike noticed a friend standing in line at a sandwich cart. He went over to greet her and meet her friend, Jennifer Wagner. It was a quick conversation, but Doug knew right away he wouldn't mind talking to Jennifer more.

After the game, the foursome met again at a bar in the Civic Center. Doug's hunches were right. Jennifer was just as nice as she seemed to be two hours ago when she made her first impression.

That was the beginning of a dating relationship that lasted more than a year. They often joked about being the country boy and the city girl. As Jennifer liked to say, she was raised on concrete in Louisville. Doug was a farm boy from Nicholas County. Actually, Doug said he was a country "man." After all, he was 30 years old when they met. She was 26.

The pairing just seemed right. Doug and Jennifer had a big church wedding in Louisville a year and a half after he first spied her from the escalator. Now, he was on another ride, this time going up.

The couple enjoyed each other's company exclusively for nearly four years, taking vacations to Cancun, then Bermuda and Montreal. It seemed neither of them had a care in the world as they hopped on planes, strolled on beaches and sampled exotic cuisine. They were yuppies with good jobs and the freedom to roam. She worked as a high school special education teacher, meaning she had summers off. He was a civil engineer, helping design things such as drainage systems for highways. Life was good, but after a while, it began to seem incomplete.

When Jennifer found out she was pregnant, she instantly kicked into that mommy-to-be mode. The anticipation of motherhood overwhelmed her. The house was baby-proofed and a nursery was ready months before the due date.

On a Sunday afternoon outing, Jennifer and Doug picked out a name for their baby. They walked a trail at Blue Licks Battlefield State Park, just four miles from Doug's boyhood home. Monuments there list the names of pioneers who tried to defend the region from British soldiers during the American Revolution. Daniel Boone was one of them.

As they scanned one marker, Doug's eyes stopped on the name "Jarrett." He remembered that someone in his family tree had that name two or three generations ago.

"Do you like that name?" he asked Jennifer.

"Very much," she said.

And that was it. It's a good thing they had a boy. Jarrett was the only name they had in mind after that.

Their pioneer namesake arrived April 16, 1989 by Caesarean section after 17 hours of labor. He was right on time, all eight pounds, eleven ounces of him.

Doug remembers the newness of bringing a baby into the house for the first time.

"We sat his carrier up on the dining room table and we both just stood there staring at him. Then we looked at each other and said 'What do we do now?'"

Is anyone ever really prepared for parenthood? Like all new parents, the Mynears became quick experts by on-the-job training. They learned one thing early on. God had blessed them with a happy baby.

Other parents had told them horror stories about babies that cried and screamed all through the night. That was never much of a problem with Jarrett. He usually slept peacefully and when awake, he smiled easily and often.

Everyone likes to brag that they have smart kids, but the Mynears had the evidence to back it up. Jarrett started talking at eight months when he surprised his parents by pointing and asking for a 'nana' at breakfast. By ten months, he was forming partial sentences. At one year, he could carry on a conversation.

At his 18-month checkup, the pediatrician told the Mynears their son had the vocabulary of a four-year-old.

Doug laughed at how other parents reacted around Jarrett.

"They would have kids that were a year older than him and Jarrett could talk rings around them. They'd look at their kids as if to say 'what's wrong with you?'"

Jarrett's parents said he was attracted to books immediately. They read to him as soon as he was big enough to sit in their laps. For many kids, a bedtime story is a nightly ritual. For Jarrett, being read to was a morning, noon and night thing. He was always crawling across the floor, dragging a book along beside him, looking for someone to translate the words and pictures.

Jarrett was around adults all the time and that no doubt boosted his development.

In the first year of his life, the infant spent a lot of hours in hospital rooms as Jennifer visited her dying father, a victim of colon cancer.

"My dad was very intolerant of kids and their antics by that time," she said, "but there was no problem bringing Jarrett into his room. Jarrett would sit on the mattress as Dad read to him and gave him rides up and down on the mechanical bed. I think Jarrett picked up a lot of words then."

He also became a baseball fan before the age of one. Doug could hold up a baseball card and Jarrett would call out the name of the team that claimed the featured player.

"Yankees!"

"Dodgers!"

"Reds!"

That was another trick that impressed his doctors.

When Jarrett could toddle enough to get out of the house, his quests were almost always in search of conversation. A neighbor remembers looking up from beyond her backyard fence one day to see Jarrett, in a diaper, pulling himself up on the deck railing to get a better look at her.

"Holly," he called out in his tiny voice. "You look like you could use some company!"

Holly just shook her head and laughed. The next thing she knew she was engaged in friendly banter with a munchkin.

3
Pleasure and Pain

"Football Weather." That's how our meteorologist summed up such nights and we all knew what he meant. Anyone going out would need a jacket or sweater but they wouldn't be too uncomfortable huddled with others in bleachers.

Jennifer and Doug put a coat on their two-and-a-half-year-old son and went to a game. As a part-time special education teacher at Lexington's Paul Laurence Dunbar High School, Jennifer wanted to show her support for the team. Besides, high school games in Central Kentucky are social gatherings–something to do on a Friday night. The Bulldogs' opponent that night was a state powerhouse, Campbell County. During the game, the couple spent some time actually watching the 22 young men go up and down the field. But their attention was divided among friends in the stands and Jarrett's wide-eyed wonder at everything else going on around him. He watched the mascots, the cheerleaders and the people who kept coming over to make small talk.

Who won the game? The Mynears' memory is cloudy on that. It's not important, because when the final horn sounded, it marked the beginning of turmoil in their lives.

As the threesome stepped out of the bleachers and onto the cold ground, Jarrett looked up at Doug.

"Daddy, carry me. My leg hurts."

That was unusual. Jarrett liked to take his parents by the hands and do his own walking. Like all kids, sometimes he'd try to break away and run off in a different direction.

Doug, who figured his son was just tired from all the excitement, hoisted Jarrett into his arms and carried him to the car, strapped him in the back seat and drove home. Jarrett didn't say another word that night about feeling pain.

In Heaven, every day must be like a late September day in the bluegrass. Many of those days are just right–not too hot, not too cold. The rustling leaves, the light breezes, and the vibrant colors of the

12

sky and trees in the early stages of change all combine for a few days to make life picture-perfect.

The day following the football game was like that. Doug spent the afternoon playing T-ball with Jarrett and Chelsea, the little girl who lived next door. They ran around in the backyard, wrestled and played tag for a couple hours. Then, all of a sudden, Jarrett once again told his dad that his leg hurt.

"He wasn't crying," Doug said. "He just mentioned it was bothering him."

His parents decided Jarrett should take it easy the rest of the weekend. They weren't too alarmed but agreed if the boy's leg still nagged him on Monday, they'd have their pediatrician check it out.

The next morning, the Mynears wanted to take Jarrett to see his grandmother, who lived 70 miles away in Louisville. Granny Jeanne, as Jarrett called her, woke early to spend the morning standing over the stove, preparing one of those Sunday meals grandmas do best. It would be a menu of comfort foods prepared in a kitchen perfumed with hot rolls and warm cookies. Granny couldn't wait to see her pride and joy and she was eager to see how her daughter was "filling out." Jennifer had recently given her mother the good news that a second grandchild was on the way.

Jennifer bounced into Jarrett's room to get him ready for the trip. She pulled the covers off the little rascal and lifted him from the bed. As soon as she touched his feet to the floor, Jarrett let out a scream. Chills shot through Jennifer. It was if someone had jumped out at her in a dark alley. Goosebumps broke out on her arms.

She could tell by the look on Jarrett's face something was terribly wrong. His smile had turned into a scowl. She sat him back on the bed and for just the third time in three days Jarrett said simply, "My leg hurts."

"I'll never forget it," Jennifer said. "I felt his right shin and it was as hot as fire."

She got to a phone quickly and called their pediatrician. Because it was a Sunday, he wasn't in his office but he agreed to meet them there, if they'd first go to Central Baptist Hospital for x-rays.

So, the couple did what the doctor advised and they all got together a couple of hours later. A quick exam of Jarrett had the doctor perplexed. It didn't appear any bones were broken or fractured, but he too felt the heat on the toddler's skin. His worst fear was that there was a bone infection. A little dark spot could be seen on the transparency.

"We were freaking out," Jennifer said. "Something in me, I guess a mother's intuition, told me it was serious. I was terribly frightened."

The pediatrician once again suggested a trip back to Central Baptist, this time for a blood test and a bone scan.

"I understood why he had wanted an x-ray," Doug said. "But a blood test? That didn't make sense to me."

The doctor went with them on the second trip.

"They had a little trouble finding a vein for the blood test, so they stuck Jarrett more than once," recalled Doug. "I was getting a little testy, wondering why they were doing this to a two-year-old– all that poking and prodding. But Jarrett never made a sound."

After the bone scan, the family pediatrician conferred with other doctors for what seemed to be hours.

To kill the time and search for comfort, Jennifer spent much of the afternoon making telephone calls from the hospital. Word spread quickly among the family's many friends and relatives that Jarrett was undergoing tests. Jennifer needed people to help keep her mind occupied and away from her worst fears. She still hadn't fully come to terms with her father's death 15 months earlier. And she was two months into a complicated pregnancy. She wasn't sure she could deal with any more bad news.

Some of the people she called showed up at the hospital to offer moral support. All of them tried to be optimistic.

Jarrett's granny walked away from her Sunday dinner for four and drove to Lexington.

Finally, the medical professionals called the Mynears into a conference room, but they still had no clear idea as to what might be in Jarrett's leg. One thought it was indeed a bone infection. Another thought it was a tumor. They all agreed that a bone biopsy was needed first thing in the morning.

Monday again found the Mynears sitting for hours in a waiting room as Jarrett went under the knife.

"I remember Doug sitting there trying to read the doctors faces as they walked past the door," Jennifer said.

"He said, 'It doesn't look like they're going to give us bad news.' I wanted to believe him, but I couldn't.

"Finally, late in the afternoon, one of the doctors came out and said 'There's good news and bad news. The good news is Jarrett made it through the surgery just fine. The bad news is there is a malignant tumor. We're 90 percent sure it's Ewing's sarcoma.'"

Jennifer felt the color flush from her face. Doug slumped down in his chair, feeling as if a heavy weight had just crashed down on his shoulders. The two never felt so weak. In the coming months, they couldn't have been more strong.

Jarrett at age 20 months

4
Diagnosis

Ewing's sarcoma is one of those mystery diseases. Medical experts don't know exactly what causes it. It's a bone cancer that's genetic but not hereditary.

The Mynears had no idea what the doctors were talking about when they mentioned the disease. There was just one pamphlet at the hospital entitled "Childhood Cancers" and it contained one sentence about Ewing's sarcoma. Later that night, the Mynears would go through a frantic and somewhat futile search for information at home, checking a medical dictionary and health-related software they had loaded on their computer.

Normal human cells contain 23 numbered pairs of chromosomes. In Ewing's sarcoma tumors, a piece of chromosome 11 has moved to chromosome 22, creating a new piece of DNA. Researchers know this so-called translocation often happens at a time of rapid growth. Children seem to be most vulnerable for tumor development in their teenage years, although it's an extremely rare condition at any age.

Jarrett's doctors quickly discovered that he was one of the youngest people to ever develop the disease.

Ewing's sarcoma starts in the bone or soft tissue, usually in the pelvis or the thigh. Even a very small tumor can lead to a microscopic spread of the cancer. Therefore, the disease requires treatment to the whole body.

Dr. Jeffrey Parr, an orthopedic surgeon in Lexington, told the Mynears on that manic Monday that he wanted them to go to the Mayo Clinic to confirm his diagnosis. Parr had done his residency there and knew how to get Jarrett a quick appointment and whom he should see once he got there.

"We felt like we'd hit rock bottom," Jennifer said. "We were willing to do anything the doctors suggested and the Mayo Clinic seemed like the best thing to do.

"But I just knew deep down inside what we were hearing meant amputation at the very least."

17

By noon Wednesday, the family van was packed and the Mynears were on the road for a 14-hour drive to Rochester, Minnesota. The most important cargo, besides Jarrett of course, was a folder containing copies of the x-ray films and bone scans and slides of the tumor cells. During the long drive, Jarrett sat obliviously in the back seat, enjoying the passing scenery. Each time Jennifer looked back at him she couldn't help but think they were taking their lamb to the lions.

They pulled into the parking lot of a Rochester motel at 2 a.m. As they stepped out of the car, the September air gave the threesome a cold welcome. In just five sleepless hours, they would have to be at the famous clinic. Doug and Jennifer felt as if their son were a defendant on trial, due in the courtroom first thing in the morning. The jury was set to consider the evidence. And even though little Jarrett had done nothing wrong, his parents knew the verdict could be devastating.

The Mayo Clinic operates with a team of two thousand physicians and sees more than a half million patients each year. Its excellent reputation for medical research is known around the world. But you aren't sent there for minor operations. If you're advised to go to Mayo, it's usually because your condition is so rare or so serious that your local doctors don't feel comfortable handling it alone.

"It's easy to see how people get intimidated there," Jennifer said. "That first morning, we walked into a conference room to face an entire disciplinary team–a prosthetist, a physical therapist, oncology nurses, a child psychologist and social workers–all sitting there around a big conference table. We were overwhelmed.

"But as soon as the discussion started, we realized they were all there to help us. They made us feel as comfortable as humanly possible at such a stressful time. It was not impersonal at all and we realized we needed to do whatever they advised."

For the next several hours, Jarrett was put through the wringer again. Even though the Mynears had the pathology slides and the x-rays from Lexington, the Mayo Clinic doctors wanted to repeat many of the tests. They started with a blood test, then a computerized tomography (CT) scan and a MRI.

"It was the oddest thing," Jennifer said. "From the beginning,

Jarrett never cried. It was like an adventure for him. And that's not selective memory. The doctors were fascinated with his reaction."

Jarrett lay still as clinic aides strapped him to tables and poked him with needles. He just watched with curiosity as the modern medical machinery passed over his body, taking pictures of his insides. Just before Jarrett came into the CT scan room, another child had to be removed because he was kicking and screaming frantically. That boy's parents decided to schedule the procedure for another time when perhaps their young patient would be calmer and less frightened.

Jarrett's parents knew that despite the dreadfulness of the situation, they had a lot for which to be thankful. Their son's demeanor took the edge off a lot of difficult decisions.

"Jarrett could be hyper," Doug said. "But he was very workable. When he knew he had to lie still, he would. We never had to tell him twice."

Doctors said it was remarkable that at his age Jarrett didn't have to be put to sleep for the magnetic resonance imaging. Even though the MRI process is painless, children–and adults, for that matter–often feel claustrophobic as their body slides on a platform into the tube-shaped scanner. Any little wiggle could distort the final images.

The magnet can also emit loud banging and knocking noises that can cause people to flinch. But Jarrett stayed as still as a guard at Buckingham Palace.

Because of her pregnancy, Jennifer wasn't able to go into a lot of the examination rooms as Jarrett went through the battery of tests. So, as Doug went from room to room with the doctors, she sat in the waiting room watching the second hand on a wall clock tick away the hours. She gazed at magazines but didn't really comprehend the articles. This wasn't like it had been in Lexington earlier in the week. Friends and relatives didn't surround her. She felt extremely lonely.

As it got darker outside, the doctors decided Jarrett had had enough for one day. They already had enough information to confirm the Kentucky diagnosis. This was indeed a case of Ewing's sarcoma. The doctors said they had one more procedure to do and then they'd let the family leave to go get some rest in their motel room.

Jennifer knew Doug had to be exhausted from being escorted all around the clinic for hours, so she told him she'd go with Jarrett for the final test. Admittedly, Doug was relieved to get a break and he knew his wife would feel better about the situation if she spent some more time with Jarrett's doctors and nurses.

But neither of them was prepared for what happened next. They assumed it was going to be another blood test or some little end-of-the-day evaluation.

"They told me to lay Jarrett down on his stomach," Jennifer said. "Then they said I'd have to hold his arms and lay my body down on his."

She was horrified to see them bring out a long hollow needle. They told her they needed to draw bone marrow from his pelvis. Jarrett was not sedated.

"Supposedly, it was easier on young patients not to take the time to knock them out," Jennifer said. "And they said someone that young can't always handle the heavy drugs it would take to ease the pain."

When the needle went into his pelvis, Jarrett broke his silence. The young man who had been a model patient all day let out a piercing scream. Then, a dam of emotions burst.

"He started to wail at the top of his lungs and squirm violently," Jennifer said. "The nurses were yelling at me to hold him still. I started to cry and it was the worst feeling I've ever had. I knew my baby was in pain and I was allowing it to happen."

The door to the exam room was shut tight, but Doug could hear the commotion as he sat waiting on the other side. He jumped up and yelled frantically through the door, "What's going on in there?"

"Let me in... let me help... somebody tell me something!"

After the marrow was collected, Doug was allowed into the room. Mother, father and son embraced in a group hug–three bodies shaking, three pairs of eyes wet.

It had to be done. They knew that. But they couldn't help feeling a little mad–mad at the doctors, mad at the world, maybe even mad at God.

As they packed up to leave for the evening, the Mynears picked up a Polaroid picture taken of Jarrett that morning. He was wearing hospital scrubs and smiling the biggest smile you've ever seen. That was the image they wanted to carry home in their minds that night.

5
60 Days

The next days at the Mayo Clinic had to be better than Day One. Most of the tests were over. Now it was just a matter of outlining the treatment.

The Mynears already knew Jarrett would have to go through chemotherapy. But they spent most of a week in meetings, learning exactly how the process would work, how much it would cost, how Jarrett's diet would change and what medications he would receive.

It's difficult to describe a roller coaster unless you've been on one. You know it goes up and down, fast and slow, but until you've felt your stomach in your throat and the breath knocked out of you, you really have no idea what the ride is like.

The Mynears were on an emotional roller coaster and each time they thought things were looking up, the track twisted, plunging them again into a tunnel or turning their outlook upside down.

When they went to their motel room after the second day at the clinic, they found a blinking red light on the telephone, meaning they had a message. They dialed a special code to hear what was recorded.

"Doug, Jennifer," said the voice from a friend back home, "I know you've got a lot on your mind and I hate to tell you this, but you need to know. The front door of your house is wide open and there's a knife in the deadbolt. Someone broke in last night."

The roller coaster knocked the wind out of them again.

The frustration and helplessness the Mynears felt by their son's illness was now compounded with a feeling of violation. Were they going to have to endure the trials of Job? It's been said God never gives you more than you can handle, but the Mynears were beginning to wonder.

They called the friend back home who described the scene. The intruder had tried to chop the deadbolt out of the front door. When that didn't work, he or she had apparently kicked the door down. Inside their home, every drawer to every desk, cabinet and dresser had been ransacked.

21

After a few minutes of collecting their wits about them, the couple began placing calls to family members, spending much of the evening making arrangements for their home to be secured. Of course, they told each other it wouldn't matter if all their possessions were gone. What really mattered was in that hotel room–mother, father, son and baby-to-be.

Even years later, they weren't able to determine if anything was actually stolen. Cameras, television sets and jewelry were left untouched. No one was ever arrested. There was no clue as to why the burglar tore through their belongings. But the Mynears had to stay in Minnesota twelve more days and all that time they were nervous about what they'd find when they returned home.

On the third day at Mayo, the feared announcement came. Option A was also Option B, C and D. The doctors said, with finality, that the only way to get rid of Jarrett's cancer was to administer chemotherapy and take off his right leg from the knee down. Other options open to older patients weren't available for Jarrett. Radiation of the tumor site would've killed the growth plates in his leg, freezing it permanently to the size of a two-year-old. And limb-sparing replacement surgery wasn't an alternative for someone who'd barely begun to grow.

Jennifer's intuition was right, but it was still difficult to hear that actual surgery was imminent. Doctors arranged for Jarrett to come back in two months for an amputation.

The first item of the seventh day was to put the youngster into surgery so a catheter could be inserted under his skin. The quarter-sized disc, known as a port-o-cath, would supply an opening for a needle in the boy's abdomen, sparing his veins from repeated stabbings.

As she waited for Jarrett to come out of the recovery room, Jennifer began to think about all the gifts her son had received at the beginning of the week when he first went in for tests in Lexington. She knew more would be coming. Everyone who knew Jarrett loved him and they wanted to make him feel better. Of course, toys and trinkets, cards and candy would do that.

"I knew it would be hard to maintain some kind of discipline," Jennifer said. "I didn't want to deny him anything, but I also didn't want him to become a spoiled brat. And I didn't want him to use his condition to get his way."

When Jennifer and Doug met with a child psychologist at the clinic that day, Jennifer expressed her concern that Jarrett might feel sorry for himself and become a source of pity. She worried that too much sympathy might make him manipulative or cause him to give up fending for himself.

The psychologist asked to spend some time with Jarrett and was granted a one-on-one appointment that afternoon.

After spending about a half-hour with the boy, the counselor came out and had a simple but profound statement for his parents: "*He's* going to be the one to get *you* through this. I can tell from his determination and intelligence that he's going to be the strong one. You have nothing to worry about."

Relief washed over the Mynears like a spring rain.

During the next week at the clinic, bone experts fitted Jarrett with a leg brace that went from the heel of his right foot all the way to the top of his hip. They said the tumor in his fibula had grown, making his leg extremely fragile. The hard plastic brace immobilized the leg so Jarrett couldn't bend his knee or put his full weight down on that foot. The boy had to learn to walk by swinging the brace in a large arc, then taking a normal step with his left leg. At first, straight paths were nearly impossible, but he took the new stride in stride, again showing pride in the way he could tackle a challenge.

The day before leaving the hospital, Jarrett had his first chemotherapy treatment. He sat for hours as poison dripped into his little veins, killing cancerous cells and growth cells, too.

That liquid trickling down the intravenous tube was the real burglar in the Mynears' lives. It was robbing their son of a normal childhood, taking away so much more than any two-bit vandal could ever steal from their house. But the droplets also carried hope, an expectation that the cancer was being stopped in its tracks.

Jennifer and Doug watched as Jarrett took it all in, asking questions about the "stuff" the nurses kept pouring in the bottles connected to the tube that went into his body.

"What's that?"

"How much do I need?"

"Will it make me pee?"

He greeted everyone who came into the room with a smile and gave them a cheerful wave when they went away. The child psychologist was right. This kid wasn't about to be robbed of his spirit.

Jarrett vomited in the hospital room that night and again after breakfast the next morning. But it wasn't a prolonged reaction. Experts say children generally tolerate chemotherapy better than adults do. Most times in the months after that, the boy showed no signs of sickness after a treatment.

Following the failed attempt to give Jarrett some food for the road, the Mynears packed up the van and headed home to Kentucky. They'd been away two weeks that seemed like two months. They were road warriors returning from battle, but the war was just beginning.

Mommy and Daddy had 60 days to prepare their son for the loss of his leg and what would become routine hospital stays. They would also have to prepare themselves.

6
Amputation

October brought some nice days to Central Kentucky, sunny afternoons when father and son could stroll outside. As Jarrett kicked at the leaves on the ground, Doug couldn't help but think this would be the last autumn for that. Even though his boy was hindered by a brace, he could still move at a pretty quick pace, sending neatly piled leaves into fluttering disarray. It was fun to watch.

When November snow covered the ground, the boy's footprints in the yard made a trail of tears for his parents. It wasn't as if Jarrett would never walk again. His parents knew he would, but it wouldn't be his real right foot trampling the blankets of white.

Jarrett lost all his hair before Thanksgiving, but that didn't seem to bother him. He thought he looked like the Kung Fu masters he saw on TV.

Doug and Jennifer talked to their son about the pending amputation and tried to be as upbeat as possible. They told him how it would take the hurt away and get all the cancer out of his body, that he would be healthy again and that it wouldn't stop him from doing anything he wanted to do in life. They told him he would be *unique* and that other kids would be amazed by his artificial leg. And most importantly, they kept a notebook for Jarrett, writing down any questions he wanted to ask the doctors.

They were the kind of questions you would expect a kid to ask:
1. *How are they going to cut off my leg?*
2. *What kind of tools will they use?*
3. *What will they do with my leg?*

The third question made Doug and Jennifer laugh out loud. They wanted to know about things such as infection and painkillers. Their son wanted to make sure his leg wasn't going to be turned into a lamp.

Jarrett's treatment protocol called for a chemotherapy session every three weeks. The Mayo Clinic arranged for those to take place at the University of Kentucky Hospital. It was a routine that would

25

continue for a year. Doctors said that's how long it would take to make sure the boy's body was cancer-free.

Just after Thanksgiving, the Mynears headed for Rochester, Minnesota again, this time taking a free flight offered by Continental Airlines.

A shuttle picked them up at the airport and took them to a nicer hotel much closer to the clinic. All of the arrangements were better this time. Jarrett was now a known client of the highly respected Mayo Clinic and provisions had been made to make his second visit as comfortable as possible.

But the welcome still seemed unfriendly, not because of the people but because of the circumstances. Doug remembered how dreary the sky seemed.

"There was a foot of snow on the ground and the wind chill was 40 below," he said.

"We would've rather been anywhere else. It was a tough thing knowing our son was coming here to be changed forever."

The next day they met Dr. Michael Rock, the orthopedic surgeon who would perform the amputation. He came equipped with impressive credentials but Doug wasn't sure he liked him.

"He didn't make a great first impression," Doug said. "He seemed so businesslike and stern. We weren't sure he could relate to plain folks from Kentucky."

Dr. Rock was indeed all business when he first consulted with the threesome. "Cut and dry" is how Jennifer would describe it.

"He was talking directly to Doug and me. There was no interaction with Jarrett at all. In the middle of the appointment, Jarrett decided he'd had enough.

"He was very articulate. We wanted him to show good manners but we understood when he spoke up and said, 'Hey, I'm the one having my leg cut off. You need to talk to me!'"

The outburst caught Dr. Rock by surprise. He hadn't meant to slight the patient. He just wasn't used to children under the age of three paying such close attention to discussions of medical procedures.

"Dr. Rock turned around and looked straight at Jarrett," Jennifer said. "I thought things were about to get tense. I figured he'd say

'Son, mind your own business. I'm talking to your parents.'

"Instead, he apologized and told Jarrett he made a good point. Then he went through Jarrett's list of questions, answering each one in a way a child could understand. From that day on, they were the best of buddies. Jarrett had input in all the meetings after that."

Doug's concerns also disappeared almost immediately.

"Our initial view of Dr. Rock was wrong," he said. "He was great through the whole thing."

It was learned that just prior to Jarrett's visit to Mayo for the surgery, he may have been exposed to chicken pox. So this stint was going to be lonelier. Even though he showed no signs of the childhood virus, he would have to stay in isolation, away from other kids and out of the playroom. He couldn't even be taken into the hallways.

But toys came to the room, wrapped in plastic. Jarrett passed the hours in a fantasy world of his own, playing with action figures and model cars, building towers with blocks and filling the pages of coloring books. When the toys went back to the playroom, they were sterilized.

"When the day of surgery came, we thought we were ready for it," Jennifer said. "But...," she paused, her voice breaking up, "... there's no way to describe what goes through your mind when you're going into the operating ward."

"That was the first time it really, I mean *really,* sunk in for me," Doug said. "You keep thinking things will change."

Jarrett was given a hospital gown and slippers. Aides wheeled him away on a gurney, as his parents watched from their seats in a waiting area, not taking their eyes off the procession until it rounded a corner out of their view.

A few minutes later, an aide came back, carrying one slipper–the one Jarrett wouldn't need for a right foot. She handed it to Jennifer, who immediately broke down in tears. She leaned her head over on Doug's shoulder and then he lost it, too.

Imagine the scene as a bystander. Here was a couple distraught, caught up in a deeply personal, emotional moment. You have no idea what the pregnant woman and her husband are going through, but

27

you feel your eyes also tearing up. You wish you could say something to make it better, but nothing comes to mind. You hurt for them. The air is heavy with sadness. The man's shirt is wet from his wife's sobs.

"It was the only insensitive thing we experienced there," Jennifer said. "I wish they had kept that slipper."

After a grueling three-hour wait, the parents were allowed to see their son. He was asleep, covered with a blanket. Again, like so many times before, Jennifer and Doug told themselves they could handle what they were about to see.

"But when they pulled the blanket down and the leg was missing, it was another emotional round for me," Jennifer said.

She wondered just how much water could be left in her tear ducts.

Doug spent the night at the hospital, holding Jarrett's hand and listening to his steady breathing. The boy was "conked out," heavily medicated with morphine for pain relief. Jennifer tried to get some sleep at the hotel. Easier said than done.

The next night, it was Jennifer's turn to stay at the hospital. The hours were long and boring, as she lay on a cot staring at the ceiling, tracing the plastered patterns with her eyes. She munched on candy as her mind swirled with thoughts about what lay ahead for her son.

"I want some of those Junior Mints."

A squeaky whisper broke the silence.

Jennifer looked over at the bed and Jarrett was looking back, wide awake and smiling. His first concern was his hungry stomach, not his missing leg.

The operation was a through-the-knee disarticulation. The surgeons didn't separate bone, just muscle and ligaments. That way when the lower leg was removed, there was no jagged bone left.

Jarrett had been fitted with a cast that went over the part of his leg that remained. It had a metal joint on the end, a place to affix a prosthesis.

After he downed his Junior Mints and enjoyed some kisses and cuddling from his mother, Jarrett suddenly seemed to become aware for the first time that his body wasn't the same as it had been two days earlier.

"He was upset when he kicked the covers down," Jennifer said. "He thought his leg was folded up in the cast. I had to remind him that his leg was gone and that he'd see that when the cast was removed."

The experts didn't make a permanent prosthesis at first because of the swelling. The artificial leg was crude to say the least, fashioned out of plastic PVC pipe, the kind you use to run water lines into your house.

On the third day after the surgery, the nurses brought Jarrett a tiny walker and he took his first steps on the plastic leg. He was totally off his pain medication then and eager to move around his room. Again, he saw it as a challenge. His parents gave him applause and encouragement with each step and Jarrett ate it up. It was like a child showing off when he first learns to ride a bike or stand on his head.

"We told him how proud we were," Jennifer said. "And we meant it."

Again, they had evidence all around them to illustrate how well Jarrett was adapting to the circumstances. A teenage girl at the clinic had gone in for the same surgery at the same time as Jarrett. She too had lost a leg to Ewing's sarcoma. She was still bed-ridden and taking heavy doses of morphine when Jarrett was shuffling around his room, demonstrating his new way of walking to anyone who would watch.

Because of the chicken pox scare, Jarrett couldn't take long strolls during the day. He still had to stay isolated in his room. But each night for the next week, his dad carried him up a back stairway to the psychiatric ward. An empty hallway there gave the young man all the room he needed to practice stepping out.

Physical therapists came in during the day, giving Jarrett an exercise regimen. The temporary artificial leg didn't bend, so they knew it would take time for the boy to really get the feel of it and find his balance.

"They said he'd need the walker for three months," Jennifer said. "But three weeks later, he put that walker in a corner and never used it again."

Two days before Christmas, Jarrett got to leave the Mayo Clinic. He had to be home in time for Santa Claus.

The hospital staff, still concerned that Jarrett may carry the chicken pox virus, cleared the hallways so the boy could be taken to the checkout desk. As his wheelchair turned a corner, Jarrett spotted a familiar face.

He yelled, at the top of his lungs, "There's the man who cut my leg off!"

Nurses popped their heads out of doorways, obviously alarmed.

Then Jarrett put on the biggest smile he could muster and waved his hand wildly.

"Hey, Dr. Rock. Good to see you!"

The hallway echoed with laughter.

7
Adjustment

Christmas at Granny's house in Louisville was "Jarrett's Day." There's no doubt about it. He was the center of attention.

Jennifer's twin brothers, Chris and Mike, whom she described as "trying to be tough and macho," softened quite a bit when they saw Jarrett. They showered their nephew with gifts and tried their best to act as if nothing had changed. They wrestled with the boy, gave him piggyback rides and sat with him to watch the holiday football games on television, explaining the plays to him and telling him when they thought the referees had made a bad call.

Everyone encouraged Jarrett to show off how well he could get around with his prosthesis. And he was happy to oblige. Of course, the living room was an obstacle course, with a large Christmas tree and stacks of gifts to maneuver around, but Jarrett did it again and again and basked in the applause and praise each time.

Granny had made more cookies than usual and Jarrett was allowed to have as many as he wanted. And throughout the day, he talked about his visit the night before from Saint Nick.

Jarrett hadn't been able to go the mall to see Santa that year and that concerned him greatly. His mother assured him that his wish list made it to the North Pole anyway, but, in true fashion, Jarrett would've liked to have spoken to the man directly.

On Christmas Eve, as the family made last minute preparations for the trip to Granny's house, there was a knock at the door of their Lexington home. The jingling of bells could be heard on the porch. Jarrett's parents told him to go see who was there.

When he opened it, he let out a cry of delight. Santa Claus stood there, with gifts in his arms.

"I knew you couldn't come see me this year, so I came to see you," Santa said. "I know you've been a very good boy."

Santa sat in a big chair in the living room and Jarrett climbed onto his lap.

"Thank you for coming," Jarrett said. "I knew you wouldn't forget me."

31

Doug's best friend, David Crowell, had arranged for a co-worker to don the red suit and he looked great in the fake beard and shiny boots. It seemed so real that even the adults half expected to see reindeer on the lawn.

Everyone watched intently as Jarrett pulled the wrapping and bows off each gift. The comfort and joy the family felt reminded them more than ever that Christmas was a time of miracles.

The prayer before the big turkey dinner the next day touched each person around the table. It was a "thank you" to God, for a child born more than two thousand years ago, and for the child in the room.

In the months that followed, Jarrett had a visit to the UK Children's Hospital every third weekend, continuing his chemotherapy treatments. Doug and Jennifer would switch off each trip, which required going in on Friday and staying overnight.

Jarrett was at the clinic in between chemo treatments too, for physical therapy, blood counts and transfusions. Doug's father Jim, known to Jarrett as "Paw," became a well-known figure around the pediatric ward. He would go with Jennifer every time, helping carry Jarrett from the car and into the treatment rooms. The boy was getting heavy and Jennifer had another child on the way.

The stress of the previous months really began to wear on Jennifer that spring. Her pregnancy caused great discomfort and she didn't sleep well. The thought of another impromptu rush to the hospital was extremely unsettling. So, her doctor scheduled a C-section for March 4, 1992, taking the guesswork out of when and where the birth would take place. Any structure in life was good at this point.

So that day, Jarrett became a big brother. His sister Claire entered the family. But he wasn't there to greet her when she came home for the first time. He was back at the clinic with his dad. It was a chemo weekend.

At that point, Doug had to give Jarrett shots for ten nights in a row after each chemo treatment. They were G-CSF shots, which stands for Granulocyte Colony Stimulating Factor. The shots, which contained a blood stimulant for building up the immune system, cost $150 each but they kept Jarrett from getting infections. It made his white cell count soar so he'd be able to take the next round of chemo.

His parents and the insurance company would work out payment later. They couldn't allow themselves to think about the mounting bills right then.

Jarrett came to dread the nightly shots to the upper thigh and Doug had to bribe him to sit still.

"He had been poked and prodded so much and he just wasn't convinced that more shots would make a difference," Doug said. "I'd give him a quarter after each shot and he would accept that as proper payment."

One month after Claire's birth, Jarrett was due back at the Mayo Clinic for restaging. That meant another round of the tests they had all become so familiar with–x-rays, a MRI, CT scan and blood counts. Jennifer stayed behind with the baby while Doug, Jarrett and Paw drove to Minnesota.

It was a happy visit. All the tests came back with good results.

"It really looked like we had killed the cancer," Doug said. "We were supposed to continue with the chemotherapy until September, just in case, but it appeared everything would be a breeze after that."

The next six months did indeed seem easy compared to what they'd been through. Jarrett turned three. The chemo visits became routine. And the young man became somewhat of a star patient around the hospital.

The nurses would come running to make over him each time he checked in. They joked with him and one kept a squirt gun handy, always ready to give Jarrett a playful spray when he wasn't looking.

"They kept him keyed up while he was there," Doug said. "They were used to seeing so many scared children that Jarrett was a joy for them to work with.

"One resident even brought her husband in to meet Jarrett," Doug added. "She had been trying to convince him they should have children and she wanted him to see how much fun it was to be around Jarrett."

Jarrett wouldn't eat breakfast at the hospital. He saved his appetite. Father and son made it a ritual to go for pizza each Saturday afternoon after checkout. While eating the pepperoni and cheese treat, they'd count down how many more times they'd do the same thing.

"We really could see the light at the end of the tunnel," Doug said.

One day shortly after Claire's birth, Jennifer drove down Southland Drive in Lexington, one of the city's older business districts. She had driven the route hundreds of times but never noticed the sign before.

"ARTIFICIAL LIMBS" just jumped out at her in big block letters.

They were at a point where they had to make a decision about Jarrett's prosthesis. The crude PVC pipe had outlived its usefulness. The swelling above the right knee was down and Jarrett had healed from the amputation.

"I just pulled my car in there to talk with them," Jennifer said. "It was on a whim, but I had a lot of questions."

His parents could've worked through a hospital to get Jarrett a new leg, but the folks at Hi-Tech Artificial Limbs just seemed to be the contact they needed.

"They were a Godsend," Jennifer said. "I feel I was guided there."

It was a private place where she could take Jarrett, avoiding long hours in hospital rooms and multiple consultations with yet another team of doctors.

The experts at Hi-Tech won points with Jarrett by talking directly to his face, asking him what he'd like his new leg to be able to do.

"I want it to bend," Jarrett said. "I want to be able to sit at a table."

With his temporary leg, Jarrett had to sit on a booster seat or have his leg extended straight out on another chair. It really did limit his ability to eat with other people, to run and climb like any other three-year-old or work in his activity books while seated.

Jarrett hit it off immediately with Maurice Adkins, Hi-Tech's president, maybe because the two had so much in common. Maurice had a prosthesis too, attached at the same point on his right leg where Jarrett's limb would be connected.

"And we were both bald and we both liked old cars," said Maurice, whose office was lined with pictures of classic coupes he had refurbished.

Over the years, Maurice, a man who could've been Jarrett's grandfather, became one of his best friends. He was a confidant and a spiritual adviser.

Maurice's right leg was shattered in 1973 when he was working on the railroad near his mountain home in Pike County in the far southeastern edge of Kentucky. Two trains collided, spilling a load of lumber onto Maurice. A board pierced completely through his shin as he lay trapped underneath the crushing weight.

He had a religious conversion under that pile of boards, praying like he'd never prayed before and he's been an outspoken Christian ever since, willing to talk about his faith to anyone who would listen.

He and Jarrett had many deep discussions over the years, about life and death, business and the Bible, faith and friendship.

Not a week goes by that Maurice doesn't get together with his little buddy. For more than ten years, they've had a weekly dinner date, usually for pizza or tacos. If Jarrett was in the hospital, then they'd have their meals together there. The only time the routine was thrown off was when Jarrett was out of state for treatment. Even then, Maurice made weekly phone calls.

That's why Jennifer called her discovery of that little office on Southland Drive a "Godsend."

A leg that fit Jarrett's specifications was ordered and built in less than a month.

"When they put it on him for the first time and he sat down in a chair and it bent, he almost cried," his mother said. "He was so excited. He just kept talking about how now he could sit down like the rest of the kids."

Almost immediately, he got into running and climbing, making his parents happy and nervous at the same time.

"We thought he was active before," Jennifer said. "Now, we were about to find out what active really meant."

The chemo treatments ended in September and the family asked Jarrett how he'd like to celebrate. Not surprisingly, he wanted to meet Chip and Dale, the polite chipmunks who were central characters in many of his books and videotapes. So they dipped into a rainy day fund and cut a few corners on household expenses to make Jarrett's dream vacation possible.

It seemed as if he had stored up three and a half years worth of energy when they went to Disney World and it all came pouring out as he strolled through the Magic Kingdom. He wanted to ride every ride, see every show and shake hands with every costumed character.

It was a tiring trip for Doug, Jennifer, Granny Jeanne, Jarrett and baby Claire, but what a good kind of tired. As they rode the monorail out of the park late that night, Jarrett's head rested on his mother's arm. He fell asleep wearing plastic mouse ears and the smile of a Cheshire cat.

The next January, Jarrett went to pre-school at a local church.

"We thought it was time to get him back into a normal routine," Jennifer said. "He had been basically isolated from his peers for more than a year."

He couldn't start in August like the other children, because his chemo treatments didn't end until September. So, once again, his arrival at a new place stood out.

His parents took him to check out the school just before Christmas.

"He walked around like he owned the place," his mother said.

"He went right up to the teachers and said, 'My name is Jarrett Mynear and I'm going to be in your class.'"

"I've had cancer, but I'm better now," he added matter-of-factly.

The teachers laughed at his outgoing personality. Typically, he had dozens of questions. He wanted to know where he would sit, where he would hang his coat and keep his supplies, and what kind of snacks they served. He was clearly excited.

On the first day of the January session, Jennifer arranged with the teachers to come in with Jarrett and have a talk with the other pre-schoolers.

They explained why Jarrett didn't have much hair (it was just beginning to grow back) and why there would be days he wouldn't be able to come to school. He showed them how his leg could come off and how he could turn it around for comic effect. He was 44 months old, with a better knack for public speaking than many 44-year-olds.

"He was never ashamed of it or self-conscious," Jennifer said. "I sat there for moral support, but Jarrett really presented the lesson. He answered any questions the kids had. I wasn't worried about his social skills after that."

Jarrett truly loved going to pre-school and pouted on the days when he couldn't go. His parents had to pull him out for weeks at a time whenever there was an outbreak of chicken pox.

"We had to explain to him why it was OK for the other kids to break out in a rash but not for him," Jennifer said. "Chicken pox could've killed him."

But, except for that fear that he'd contract a childhood virus, life seemed back on track.

Jennifer went back to work part-time as a teacher at Paul Laurence Dunbar High School. It was good for her to get her mind back on her career.

Jarrett turned four, finished the spring session of pre-school, and headed back to the Mayo Clinic for his 21-month checkup.

"The doctors there were excited to see him. They went through all the tests and scans and were beaming when they gave us the results," Jennifer said.

"The word they used was 'awesome,'" she remembered. "They said there was a better than 90 percent chance Jarrett had been cured. Basically, they told us to go back to Kentucky and have a nice life."

One of the doctors came to the examining room to ask Jarrett to demonstrate how he could run down the hall for the benefit of the parents of another child facing a similar amputation.

Jarrett said he'd be glad to and he instantly kicked into a "show off" mode. He ran up and down the hall, not once but three times, making sharp turns on his heels when he changed direction and picking up speed each time, giggling all the way.

Doug and Jennifer saw relief on the faces of the mother and father who were about to send their child under the knife. Two strangers suddenly realized they could handle the ordeal they were about to confront. At that moment, their son was a counselor, providing encouragement to a man and woman desperately in need of cheer. It was a role he would take on many times in the years to come.

Jarrett spent the summer doing what four-year-olds do—drawing pictures, watching television, playing in the park and pulling pranks on his babysitters.

He completed another session of pre-school the following fall and spring. For a full year, the roller coaster stayed parked at the station. Medically, Jarrett's life was uneventful. The checkups that came every three months or so continued to bring good news. Cancer appeared to be something he had whipped.

As his kindergarten season approached, his family couldn't have known the coaster was about to plunge again.

8
The Cancer Returns

By all appearances, the Mynears had been given a fresh start. They had decided their house in Lexington was too small for their growing family and found a place they loved on an acre just two miles to the south in Jessamine County. It was near woods and fields–good places for kids to explore.

Jarrett went to kindergarten in a new place, but he didn't act like a stranger. Once again, he started the year by telling his new classmates at Rosenwald-Dunbar Elementary School about his cancer and his artificial leg. But by then, he was talking as a cancer survivor, telling them it was all gone.

"There's nothing to worry about," he told the other four- and five-year olds. "You can't catch it. It's not like the mumps or chicken pox. And even if that were possible, you wouldn't catch it from me. I don't have it anymore."

But, unknowingly, Jarrett told a lie.

One evening, about a month into the term, Doug helped Jarrett get ready for bed. As he shampooed Jarrett's hair, which was now thick and dark, he noticed a tender spot on the crown of his head.

"Ouch!" Jarrett winced, as his dad touched it again.

"He was a very active kid, so we thought he bumped it on the playground or on something at school," Doug said. "But Jarrett said he couldn't remember hitting anything with his head."

His parents checked the spot for about five days and it didn't get any better. So, experience told them they'd better see a doctor.

A trip to the UK Hospital revealed the last thing anyone wanted to hear. There was a tumor under that soft spot on Jarrett's skull.

Once again, they packed the family van and headed to the Mayo Clinic, this time with toddler Claire in tow and Granny Jeanne along to baby-sit.

"They pulled all the scans from June and it was there," Jennifer said in disbelief. "They had missed it!"

A dark spot showed up on the slides of Jarrett's skull and somehow the best doctors in the world at one of the best clinics in the world had overlooked it. The scans had been taken from the front and back of the skull, but not from the top. It's important to remember that Jarrett was one of the youngest patients ever diagnosed with Ewing's sarcoma, so there wasn't any history on how to best test for the spread of the disease in someone his age.

Typically, Ewing's goes from the arms and legs into the lungs. Over the years, doctors have learned they'd better check everywhere. Now, they always do a scan of the top of the head.

"We couldn't believe it wasn't caught," Jennifer said.

She admits she was instantly angry. How could they be going through this again? If they had noticed this four months ago, could it have been nipped in the bud?

"But after you go through being mad and settle down, you realize everyone's human," Jennifer said. "Nobody's perfect. These things happen. The past can't be changed. You just have to concentrate on what's next."

The doctors devised another treatment plan.

"The specialist on the case made the statement that he wanted to go at it full-force and get rid of this thing once and for all," Jennifer said.

"Full-force" meant a three-month regimen of super intensive chemotherapy back at UK, followed by consideration of a stem cell transplant. Jarrett was in the hospital five days at a time for these strong treatments, which again came every three weeks.

Jennifer took a leave of absence from her half-day teaching job so she could be at the hospital during those five-day stretches. Claire had to be shuttled to a babysitter every day while Doug worked, because the Mynears didn't want another child to have to spend countless hours around doctors, nurses and sick people.

Their good friend Julie Hoagland became like Claire's second mother. She was the ever-dependable babysitter, always available and never concerned about how long the family would be away.

"Julie kept me from completely losing my mind," Jennifer said. "It was hard for me to leave Claire every day, but I knew she was with someone who genuinely loved her and treated her like her own child. She was much more than just a babysitter. She was part of the family."

Doug would relieve Jennifer at the end of his workday, so the couple spent very little time together.

"We would meet for dinner in Jarrett's room and then one of us would go home with Claire and the other would stay at the hospital with Jarrett," Doug said. "It was a lonely time for all of us."

After the three months of chemo ended, doctors still had no assurance they were beating the cancer. When pressed for a prognosis, the doctors said Jarrett had about a five percent chance of living with conventional treatments. So, another big decision fell into the Mynears' laps.

"They told us the best chance for getting rid of the cancer forever was to go ahead with a stem cell transplant," Jennifer said. "And the best place for that would be the Fred Hutchinson Research Center in Seattle.

"That would mean uprooting and moving clear across the country for several months," she said. "But that's just an automatic. You do what you need to do."

Stem cell transplant. Another confusing term. They didn't like the sound of it.

Jennifer said, "We read and read until we were cross-eyed, but that still doesn't prepare you for what it really means."

Mynear family portrait: Jarrett, Claire, Doug and Jennifer

9

Sickness in Seattle

Stem cells are baby blood cells that haven't decided what they'll be when they grow up. They could become red cells (which carry oxygen around the body), white cells (which protect against infection), or platelets (which prevent bleeding).

In Jarrett's case, the doctors wanted an autologous transplant. That meant the stem cells would come from his own bloodstream. It's a less risky procedure and because Jarrett's bone marrow showed no signs of the disease, it wasn't necessary to find a donor.

The cells would be taken from a special catheter in Jarrett's chest, stored while he underwent a strong chemo session to kill his bone marrow, then returned to his body. If all worked as planned, the returned baby cells would travel through the bloodstream and find their way to the empty bone marrow spaces, where they would start to grow and develop into mature blood cells. He would be injected with growth factors to encourage the stem cells to migrate from the marrow into the bloodstream.

All the literature told the Mynears this could be highly beneficial. But they also read that the process had side effects in people who are in generally poor health and each year about one in four patients dies from the procedure.

They had faced a lot of tough decisions, but none of them had seemed to be matters of life and death. They were having brainstorms, but not the kind that reflect sudden great ideas. These were the kind of storms that cloud your thinking, give you headaches, and keep you awake at night. It was as if a flood of thoughts was rushing around in their turbulent heads, none of them solid enough to grasp.

The doctors had made a mistake months earlier when they missed the tumor on a brain scan. Now they recommended a risky transplant. Did they really know or were they guessing? Was their kid a guinea pig? A clinical trial balloon?

The doctors' voices grew stronger as they echoed in Doug and Jennifer's minds. *"Jarrett is young and active. He can fight off any side effects. The fatalities happen to those who've had much more chemotherapy and radiation. Trust us. Trust us. Trust us.*"

"We really came to the conclusion that we had no choice but to trust them," Jennifer said.

"God gave us a child to take care of and now we had to turn his well-being over to total strangers. That's where helplessness came in."

Jennifer and Doug found out what it means to be "talked out." They discussed every scenario with each other until they couldn't think of anything else to say. They prayed more than they had ever prayed. And, despite continued trepidation, the answer seemed to be clear. They would go to Seattle and once again meet more doctors they'd never seen before at another world-renown institution.

The day after Thanksgiving, the family of four boarded a plane bound for the west coast with no guarantee the Fred Hutchinson Center would even take Jarrett as a patient.

Doug brought along a laptop computer. He had arranged to transfer a lot of his work with him. It was truly amazing how understanding his employer was and how willing his bosses at Booker Associates were to work around his complicated lifestyle.

On the following Monday, the Mynears showed up at the cancer center–a pristine building in a beautiful city. It was a change in longitude and latitude, but everything else was deja vu.

Inside, it could've been Any Hospital U.S.A. The machinery looked the same, the needles were just as sharp, and the smells and noises told you this was a place for sick people. Jarrett went through the familiar battery of tests–being jabbed with syringes, scanned with magnets and photographed with bursts of radiation.

By the end of the week, the specialists there said they would admit Jarrett to the clinic and proceed with the stem cell harvest. Again, the doctors tried to assure the Mynears that this was *the* way to go.

That evening, the Kentucky clan checked into a 300-square foot efficiency apartment just a few blocks from the cancer center. It was way too crowded for four people, but the price was right and the location convenient. Anyway, Doug and Jennifer knew it would mostly be a place to sleep. They'd be at the hospital almost every waking hour.

They were used to these trips away from home being miserable. This time, Claire got the blahs. She had developed some type of breathing infection just before they left home. She sat around feeling dismal most of the time. Her parents felt helpless, wishing they could wave a magic wand and make their little girl bouncy and playful.

This initial trip to Seattle was expected to take five to seven days. Each day, Jarrett showed up to have his blood counts tested. The stem cells would be collected when everything was at the right level. He received daily shots to stimulate his white count but a week passed and it just wasn't high enough.

They stayed an extra week before doctors attempted the harvest.

On the appointed day, Jarrett stretched out on a bed in the pheresis room. Blood traveled through the catheter in his body and trickled into a centrifuge, which spun rapidly to separate the stem cells. The remaining blood returned to him through the tube in another vein. The process lasted nearly four hours, with the collected stem cells being immediately frozen. They would be saved until after Jarrett had gone through another round of high-dose chemotherapy.

But the process was only semi-successful. It didn't yield nearly enough cells. The family learned Jarrett would have to stay at the center a few more days, until his white count got high enough to try again.

After another week of low counts, the Mynears temporarily put the red light on the procedure.

"It was getting closer to Christmas and we had two kids who were getting very fidgety," Jennifer said. "They were both very much into Christmas and none of us could stand another day in that efficiency apartment.

"Friends had been sending us cards and a miniature Christmas tree that was all decorated and that just made us all the more homesick."

They flew back to Kentucky in time to spend the holiday with the whole family–grandparents, aunts and uncles, nieces and nephews. They'd try to harvest more stem cells after the new year rolled in.

Jennifer said, "We didn't know if we'd have another Christmas together. That took priority right then."

It was another great holiday for the kids. They were both

showered with love, not to mention toys, clothes and candy. But for mom and dad, there was a lot of stress under the surface.

"We knew we had to get back to Seattle and get those stem cells," Jennifer said. "We had the appointments set up, a three-month schedule of chemotherapy on the calendar and a child with a tumor on his skull. It was all we could think about."

In between preparing meals, visiting friends, giving gifts and all the other hectic, happy rituals of the season, Jarrett's parents had to book airline tickets, find a bigger apartment in Seattle and make arrangements for someone to take care of their house and bills while they would be away.

Jarrett was to return to the Fred Hutchinson Center in mid-January. In the meantime, he had to have one chemo session in Kentucky so he'd be on schedule. After the treatment and a few days before he was to go west again, there was another setback. The boy caught the flu.

Looking back, all Jennifer could say was that it was stupid not to delay the trip to Seattle. But that's 20/20 hindsight. At the time, it appeared their son could handle it and she and Doug believed the clock was ticking.

Jennifer and Jarrett went to the Lexington's Blue Grass Airport as scheduled, with Doug planning to bring Claire along in a few days.

As soon as they got in the air, Jarrett started throwing up. It was as if the flu got up to speed as soon as the commuter plane did. It was just a 15-minute flight to Cincinnati and their connection. Jennifer told herself things would be better once they got on a bigger plane. The flight would be smoother and Jarrett could sleep. She just wouldn't let him have anything to eat until they reached their destination.

It's a four-hour flight from Cincinnati to Seattle, but it seemed as if they'd never get there. Jarrett threw up again about a half-hour into the second leg of their journey and was sick the rest of the way.

"I'm still mad at myself for not seeing how ridiculous it was to get on that second plane," Jennifer said. "He got so weak and dehydrated, he just slumped over in the seat. He was as pale as a ghost. The flight attendants took turns bringing him ice and cold cloths to put on his forehead."

The attendants also sat with Jarrett if Jennifer had to go to the restroom. It was obvious to everyone on board that this was a very sick little boy. Flying exacerbates dehydration. His mother tried to get her son to drink more water, but he just spit it back up.

On the other end, hospital volunteer John Hayes waited to meet the Mynears. The cancer clinic often paired out-of-state patients with local folks who could make their visit more comfortable.

"The man who was there to greet us had to come on board and carry Jarrett off the plane," Jennifer said. "It wasn't the introduction any of us had anticipated. But Jarrett was so limp I couldn't pick him up."

They didn't bother to check into their apartment or pull over to see any sights. The welcoming committee of one rushed Jarrett straight to the emergency room, where he was immediately hooked up to intravenous fluids.

"That's the worst of all the ordeals I've been through," Jennifer said. "I was terrified. We were supposed to be there to get stem cells. Instead, Jarrett was admitted to the hospital with a violent and dangerous case of the flu.

"That's the only time I've seen him so sick he wouldn't talk to anyone. He withdrew and curled up into a ball. He wouldn't even reach for the phone when his dad was on the line."

Jennifer said she could actually hear crunching in Jarrett's lungs as he breathed. It sounded like gravel turning over in a storm drain.

The hospital booked Jarrett into a double room so his mother could stay with him. She wouldn't have thought of leaving, even if she would've had to sleep on the floor in a closet.

The next few days crept by, with Jennifer hanging on the edge of a nervous breakdown. Her husband and daughter were 2,000 miles away and her son right beside her seemed even more distant than that.

Jarrett spent the hours lying in bed, broken out in sweat, with IV tubes steadily dripping fluids into his body.

Jennifer made dozens of phone calls to Kentucky, talking to Doug, her friends, her mother, and Claire's babysitter–anyone who could help her pass the time. She knew it must be costing a fortune, but what was the price tag on her sanity? She felt she'd surely go crazy if she didn't stay connected with the world outside Jarrett's hospital room.

When she wasn't on the phone, she worked crossword puzzles and thumbed through every old magazine in the waiting rooms in that section of the hospital. But there was no satisfaction in filling in the blanks or in reading what Hollywood starlet was back on the dating scene.

Sadness had taken up residence in her mind and body. Food didn't taste good, the TV sitcoms weren't funny, the mattress was hard and the room was cold. She felt very old. It seemed the bright lights in her life had gone dim. Jarrett, whose spirit could usually outshine a lighthouse, was more like a night-light now. There was still a glow about him but right then he couldn't make the shadows disappear.

They were in a modern medical facility with an impeccable reputation. But to Jennifer, theirs was a room of gloom.

As she looked in the mirror over the sink in Jarrett's room, Jennifer knew she had to shake the blues. The dark circles under her eyes were a sign that she needed to be more concerned about her own health, both physical and mental.

"Jarrett's going to snap out of this flu in a few days," she told herself, "and he needs me to be strong and upbeat."

Jennifer gave herself a good talking-to and then picked up the phone again. She asked her mother if she could come join her in Seattle. Granny Jeanne was one step ahead of her daughter. She already had her suitcase packed.

After a week, Jarrett started to perk up a little. He was happy to see his granny and he wanted to know about other people back home.

He would sit up to watch television. He still liked Sesame Street and Barney, the purple dinosaur. And he paid attention to the local news. It helped him understand a little more about Seattle, the city outside his window.

He stayed groggy under heavy medication, but he was taking an interest in his surroundings. He was Curious George again, asking questions. The doctors thought Jarrett would make a great reporter some day. He already knew the five W's.

Who? What? Where? When? Why?

He didn't take notes, but he sure knew how to conduct an interview. His thirst for knowledge was back, keeping his mind active even when his body was too weak to stir.

The doctors decided they didn't want to delay Jarrett's cancer treatment any longer. They needed to get more stem cells so they could go ahead with the stronger doses of chemo. The tumor had to be attacked. The sooner, the better.

As the preparations were being made, an anesthesiologist came in to meet the young patient. But he called Jennifer out into the hallway after being in the room for just a few minutes.

"He told me he couldn't believe anyone would think of putting this child under," she said. "In his mind, Jarrett was still too weak. He said he didn't want to have any part in it."

Of course, that alarmed Jennifer. She already felt guilty about bringing her son to Seattle in his current condition. She didn't want to make another mistake.

On the other hand, the doctors were convinced Jarrett had seen the worst of the flu and that the stem cell procedure needed to be scheduled as soon as possible.

"I prayed a lot and decided I had to trust the doctors," she said.

When you're remodeling a house, you have to tear up to fix up. Things can sure be messy for a while, but in the end, the results are worth it. Jarrett reminded his mother of a work in progress. Evidently, he had to get worse before he could get better.

Jennifer's decision was made all the more difficult by Jarrett's appearance.

"The bout with the flu had really taken a toll on him. He had lost so much weight, he was just skin and bones," she said. "At one point, he was on oxygen."

But she could tell he was getting stronger. Perhaps the heavy doses of antibiotics had done the trick. So she allowed the doctors to go ahead and put a temporary catheter under Jarrett's collarbone–an entry point for more IV's. She'd see how he handled that surgery before she gave the OK to allow another stem cell harvest.

When Jarrett woke up on the operating table, the rigid catheter was in place, looking like a straw sticking from his neck. He seemed to come through it just fine, so the next day the doctors again hooked up the drip tube and collected stem cells. This time, they got all they needed.

The doctors decided to delay the super-strong chemo treatment for a few more weeks. They wanted Jarrett to go home to Kentucky and get tougher.

That's just what he did.

10
The Dream Factory

Before Jarrett headed back to Seattle in early March, he had another trip to make–up and down the aisles at Best Buy.

The nurses at UK had arranged for the little man to have a wish fulfilled by The Lexington Dream Factory, a non-profit organization with the sole goal of spreading joy to seriously ill children.

Jarrett, now nearly six years old, had become quite an artist on his family's personal computer. He loved to make greeting cards and posters and he had mastered the Paintbox program. But he never liked the way his works of art turned out when he ran them through the family's black and white dot matrix printer. He really wanted a color inkjet printer.

When he learned The Dream Factory wanted to let him pick out a printer at the electronics superstore, Jarrett perked up. The organization not only wanted him to get a printer, it had arranged a shopping spree. Jarrett was told he would be allowed to fill a shopping cart with any items he wanted that would help him pass the time in Seattle.

When the family showed up at Best Buy, they were greeted by three strangers: Terry Hagan, who was in charge of "dream procurement;" The Dream Factory's past president, Ralph Coldiron; and board member Leslie Beebe. They had a dolly waiting and told Jarrett to hop on and point the way. Jarrett knew right where the printers were and off he went, like a tornado on four wheels.

It was the first time a television crew was made aware of Jarrett's condition. A videographer ran along behind the dolly, capturing the excitement in Jarrett's face. A newspaper reporter kept close, too. The young man didn't mind the attention at all.

"We almost felt embarrassed that he wanted a printer," Jennifer said. "Doug and I were afraid it would look like we had asked him to get it for us. It didn't seem like the thing most kids would want, but it really was what Jarrett wanted most."

Only one would do–a high-resolution, top-of-the-line model by Epson. Terry Hagan worked for Lexmark, a Lexington-based

51

company that specializes in printers, so he made a spirited effort to sway Jarrett away from his competitor.

"Look at all this one does," Terry said, holding up a printer that came off his employer's assembly line. "Wouldn't this be a better choice?"

But Jarrett had his mind made up.

"No offense, Mr. Hagan, but if you don't mind too much, I've already studied up on the Epson."

"He started talking about pixels and fonts and resolution," Terry said. "I couldn't believe how smart he was."

Terry picked up the printer Jarrett wanted and put it on the dolly.

"You know how much trouble I'd be in if my boss saw me do this?" Terry asked, jokingly. "Get me away from here. How would you like to go get some video games?"

"Really?" Jarrett squealed with delight. "I only planned to get a printer. Are you sure it's not too much?"

"We want you to have anything you'd like," Terry said. "It's all been taken care of. Don't worry about the price."

It didn't take long for Jarrett to select a handheld Sega Game Gear system. It was just the right size to take on an airplane.

"You'd better get some games to go with it," Terry said.

Jarrett picked out a Power Rangers game and a trendy one called Sonic the Hedgehog. Terry held up four more.

"Do you think you'd like these, too?"

Jarrett nodded in disbelief and his new friend dropped them in the cart.

"We were amazed," Jennifer said. "We couldn't believe these people we didn't know cared that much about him."

Ralph Coldiron also tossed a carrying case onto the stack. In his head he had figured up that the items in the cart would come to about $900. He didn't mind pushing it to a thousand.

"You'll need to protect that game system when you're traveling," he said.

"Is there anything else you'd like?"

"No thank you," Jarrett said. "You've given me too much."

The young television reporter asked Jarrett if she could have a few words with him on camera.

"OK," he said. "No problem."

As Terry wheeled Jarrett toward the front of the store where the camera was being set up, Jarrett asked him to stop.

They were in the video aisle.

"Could I get one more thing?" he asked.

"Sure, what is it?"

"I'd like to get a movie for my sister."

Jarrett reached over to a shelf and took down a VHS tape decorated with a picture of Barney, the purple dinosaur.

"Claire would really like this."

The Dream Factory reps knew they hadn't gone wrong in selecting this kid for a treat. He was humble and grateful and unselfish. Deserving. Very deserving.

The reporter was blown away by how well Jarrett answered her questions. So were his parents. Although in the coming years, he would become a pro at television interviews, this was his first time in action. He told her why he had wanted a printer, about the stem cell transplant he would receive in the coming weeks and how he expected to be cured. And most of all, he kept saying how nice it was for the people at The Dream Factory to give him all these gifts.

"They're awesome," he said. "And they do this for other kids, too. I'm really glad I got to know them."

"He's a natural," the young lady said afterward.

======

Three months later, as Jarrett sat in the small apartment in Seattle recovering from the transplant, he took out a pen and paper. He had just celebrated his sixth birthday. Many of the cards he had received from friends and relatives contained money.

He took a ten-dollar bill and stuffed it in an envelope, along with a note scrawled in crayon.

Dear Dream Factory,
Last Feb. you gave me a shopping spree at Best Buy. I'm home from my transplant now. Use this money for someone else to get a dream come true. This is part of my birthday money.
Your friend,
Jarrett Mynear

Terry Hagan was astounded when he opened the letter and the money fell out. The Dream Factory had never had a child give back like that.

His mother said the organization taught Jarrett an important life lesson.

"He was really touched by what it had done for him and he learned how neat it is to reach out and help others," she said.

An annual donation became a tradition for Jarrett. Ten dollars always came out of his birthday money.

"I'm sure ten dollars won't buy a dream, but every dollar helps," he said. "I want them to keep up the good work."

More examples of generosity were just around the corner. Jarrett would be on both the giving and the receiving ends.

11
Difficult Journey

Jarrett's parents had been deeply moved by The Dream Factory's acts of kindness. But the shopping spree also stirred some sadness in them.

"It was a validation that we may not come home from Seattle with our son," Jennifer said. "It was like he was being granted his *last* wish. We knew we were going into a horrible, life-threatening situation."

The return to Seattle came on March 5th, one day after the family celebrated Claire's second birthday. Special days are big for many families, but this foursome valued celebrations of life even more than most.

Right after the party, Jennifer finished packing the last of the things she thought she'd need out west– clothes, kitchen utensils and toiletries. She also wanted to send a few toys and books that were familiar to her children. She expected to be away from home at least four months.

"It was hard to think about being gone that long," she said. "We wanted to go quietly to the airport and just kind of slip out of town."

But on the morning of departure, more than a dozen friends and relatives showed up at the house to show their love and support. They helped the family carry bags to the car that was waiting for them, loaded Jarrett and Claire down with snacks and magazines to enjoy on the plane, and joked with Doug and Jennifer about how they were going to redecorate the house while they were gone.

Then, there was a scene that reminded one of the receiving line at a wedding. As the foursome headed to the car, each member had to stop for handshakes, hugs and words of encouragement. Everyone was determined to get in his or her goodbyes.

As the car pulled away, the group of well wishers stood in the driveway, waving wildly. Jennifer could tell Doug was tearing up and she refused to look back again, knowing she would cry.

"I didn't want the kids to see us all weepy," she said. "We were trying to make this an adventure for them."

They held up pretty well for 20 minutes. Then, they went to their gate at the airport and found more friends waiting there.

As the plane lifted off, they looked down at the lush pastures of the Bluegrass, lined with white fences. Off in the distance, they could see the tall buildings that marked downtown Lexington. They were homesick already, but it was good to know there were people down there who would be praying for them and eagerly awaiting their return.

On this flight, there was a fifth passenger in the Mynear party—one who had never flown. Doug's mother, Mildred, insisted on going along to baby-sit Claire for a week or so while her son and daughter-in-law went through another round of meetings with doctors.

Granny Mynear lived the simple life, having grown up without running water or indoor plumbing. She had never strayed far from the farm and had never been away from Paw for more than a day in their 44 years of marriage. She found Lexington, with its 225,000 people, to be a big and sometimes scary city. She really couldn't imagine what Seattle would be like.

Doug's mother was as white as a sheet when the ground dropped out from under the plane. She didn't like one minute of the flight, but she was determined that if her grandson could go through all he was facing, she could endure the terror of being off the ground.

"It was the sweetest thing," Jennifer said. "I can't tell you how special that was to us."

To Granny Mynear, it was just a simple way to help. To her family, it was a profound act of love.

12
A Kindred Spirit

Jarrett looked forward to a reunion on the west coast. During his first trip to "The Hutch," as the Fred Hutchinson Center was often called, he made a new friend–one that was about 45 years older than him.

Just like Jarrett, Bob Hjort had crossed the country for a stem cell transplant. The native of Maine and his wife stayed in the same apartment building as the Mynears and they often passed in the halls. Bob carried a portable IV bag with him everywhere he went.

"Looks like you and I are here for the same thing," Bob said to Jarrett as they each showed up at the cancer clinic to have their blood counts taken.

That was the opening Jarrett needed. He immediately began to ask the man questions about his cancer, his family, and his home in New England.

"They hit it off instantly," Jennifer said. "Bob and his wife Anita invited us to their apartment that night and it was great to have some conversation with someone away from the hospital setting."

Bob and Anita had a Christmas tree in their apartment. That made it seem a little homier, even though the rooms were laid out exactly like the ones in the Mynears' unit. To Jarrett and Claire, a visit down the hall became like a trip to a relative's house, with different things to see and explore.

The families got together several times a week after that first visit. Within a few days, Anita hung stockings next to their tree. Two names were stitched in the fabric– "Jarrett" and "Claire."

Bob taught Jarrett to play Hearts and the man showed no mercy. He made it clear he wasn't going to let Jarrett win just because he was a little kid. That made Jarrett all the more determined to claim victory. Sometimes, he'd hide a card in his lap or under the tablecloth.

Bob would taunt him: "Cheat, cheat, never beat."

That was his chant over and over again. He'd sing it out anytime Jarrett won, even when the boy hadn't cheated. It always made

Jarrett smile.

During Jarrett's second trip to Seattle, Bob was one of the first people to get a grin out of Jarrett when he was suffering with the flu.

"Jarrett was lying there in bed, not really responding to anyone or anything," his mother recalled. "Then there was a tap outside the door."

It was Bob, carrying his IV bag and a deck of cards.

"Does anyone know where a man could find a good game of Hearts?"

Jarrett rolled over and his eyes lit up.

"You think you could beat me?" Jarrett asked, sitting up.

And the games resumed.

"Anita and I would sit and talk while the two of them played," Jennifer said. "I knew both of them were feeling miserable, but they kept each other going."

Bob also kept the family in stitches by recounting one of the unpleasant tasks of his chemotherapy. Doctors asked him to go through the distasteful routine of analyzing his own vomit and bowel movements. He had to fill out a form each time something came up or out. The form asked him to describe the texture and color of his "emissions."

"Where do they come up with these terms?" Bob asked, feigning indignation. "Foamy, creamy, soupy. Don't they know what puke looks like?"

"Eventually," Jennifer said while laughing, "he purchased a set of colored pencils and tried to match the colors in the margin of the form. We got quite a kick out of him trying to find out which two colors mixed together would best describe his stool. I guess after you've been through all we'd been through, you get a sick sense of humor."

If imitation is the sincerest form of flattery, then Jarrett paid Bob quite a compliment. Jennifer noticed one morning that Jarrett had filled out his own form after a trip to the bathroom. There were brown and yellow scribble marks in the margin, made by colored pencils.

The reunion was nice, but Jarrett didn't get to see Bob much during his third trip to Seattle. Bob had his stem cell transplant a few days before Jarrett was scheduled to have one. There were complications and Bob didn't live through it.

The Mynears kept that news from Jarrett for as long as they could, telling him that Bob just wasn't able to visit anymore.

Once again, Jarrett's parents were hit with the reality that this was a dangerous procedure. Hit hard. They watched someone they had come to love slip away in an instant.

Bob had tried to cheat death.

"Cheat, cheat, never beat."

Their son would be the next person at The Hutch to lay his cards on the table. They prayed that for once he'd be dealt a winning hand.

13
Transplant

Doug and Jennifer had never seen so much paperwork. Before the stem cell transplant could begin, they had to sign form after form, acknowledging they knew the risks their son was about to face.

"Basically, the papers said if we were lucky, our child would live," Jennifer said. "If we were *really* lucky, he would be rid of his cancer."

It was like buying a new, expensive product that came with no guarantee. No refunds, no exchanges.

"There were pages and pages of risks–everything from permanent brain damage to strokes and paralysis, not to mention death," his mother said. "We had to sign a statement that we understood this was a clinical trial. It spelled out all the positives and negatives, but the negatives seemed to go on and on.

"We read and read and searched the Internet. We talked to former transplant patients–anything and everything we could do to get more information."

But in the end, the choice was clear.

"We either had to do something aggressive or let him die."

Another week passed before the heavy chemo treatments could begin.

"The financial coordinators wouldn't even discuss proceeding until they found out if our insurance would pay," Jennifer said. They had been told the minimum tally for this hospital stay would be $150,000.

Once the insurer gave the go-ahead, Jarrett began the hardest round of chemo he'd ever endured. This would be oral chemotherapy, requiring the five-year-old to take 42 pills a day.

"Every time he turned around, it was time to take another pill," his mother said.

Besides the chemo pills, there were pills to prevent seizure, nausea and bacterial infection.

Again, Jarrett was a trooper. He did what he was told, with little complaining.

At this point, his immune system had dropped to zero. That was the reason for this round of chemo–to completely kill the bone marrow.

His parents had to relearn how to take care of their son. As his primary caregivers, they had to go to classes on how to use a portable IV pump. Soon, many of his drugs would be administered at the apartment. And they had to learn about nutrition. Jarrett's eating habits had completely changed. The list of things he couldn't have was a lot longer than the list of things that were allowed.

"We got to a point where it was a goal to get him to eat 20 Cheerios a day," Jennifer said. "We would count out maybe five at breakfast, five at lunch and ten at dinner. His stomach was rejecting almost all food. We would try to add a few bites of fruit every now and then. Sometimes it stayed down, sometimes it didn't. Most of his nutrition came through a tube."

They had to become obsessive about germs and cleanliness. Everything in the apartment had to be scrubbed with Clorox every day–the counter tops, the cabinets and floors. Laundry was an everyday chore as well.

"It was years until I could stand the smell of Clorox again," his mother said. "Our apartment smelled like a bleach factory."

During the first weeks in Seattle, Jarrett's parents liked to take him to the Seattle Arboretum. It was a beautiful place, like a peaceful Garden of Eden. But now, it was out of the question. Jarrett couldn't get dirty, couldn't breathe in pollen or be exposed to mold.

Two days after the last chemo treatment, he went into Swedish Hospital for the transplant. The hospital was partnered with The Hutch. All his mother can remember about that morning is a feeling of nausea.

"I was a nervous wreck and the room had the worst smell to it," she said. "You've never smelled anything like the preservatives they keep the stem cells in. It's a peach-colored liquid that drips into the patient's body. It's visually nauseating, too."

Half of the collected cells went into Jarrett's body and presumably straight to work, building back the marrow that had been killed.

It was to be a 17-day hospital stay, with daily blood counts. The baby stem cells were growing up, turning into white cells, fighting infection. There was medical magic taking place inside a frail little boy.

Outside Jarrett's window, Seattle lived up to its reputation as a clouded and rainy place. In Kentucky, some old-timers claim they know when rain's approaching, simply by feeling it in their bones. Jarrett's parents had a feeling about the figurative weather too. Their intuition told them sunnier days were just ahead.

14
The Pink Ladies

The view from Jarrett's hospital room was like a postcard. Swedish Hospital stands on a hill overlooking Puget Sound. Because Jarrett's parents wanted to keep his mind strong, they challenged him to imagine what was going in the world he could see outside his window.

He'd talk about the freighters coming in, trying to guess what they were hauling and what their destination would be. The large cranes that lifted cargo on and off the ships fascinated him. He dreamed up all kinds of scenarios about the men he saw walking along the docks and scurrying about the decks. Maybe some of them were pirates or spies or whalers.

Two days after his transplant, while he was gazing toward the harbor, a cart rolled into his room, pushed by two members of the hospital's auxiliary. The women looked quite cheery in their pink smocks.

Jarrett noticed right away the cart was loaded with toys.

"We didn't know anything about the toy program or the adult volunteers who made these visits," Jennifer said. "It was a nice surprise."

The ladies told Jarrett he could pick out something from the cart and keep it as their gift to him. He looked it over thoroughly, impressed with the selection of games, books, stuffed animals and puzzles. He finally settled on a piece of string art–a picture printed on a piece of cardboard that he could weave yarn through to make a colorful display. It was something that could keep his mind and fingers busy.

As the volunteers turned to leave, Jarrett thanked them and asked when they'd be back.

"Next Friday."

"I'll be here too. See you then!"

In fact, Jarrett was there long enough to get three visits from the "Pink Ladies," as he called them. They were three visits that maybe took up 15 minutes of Jarrett's life. But in those minutes, a seed was planted in the boy's fertile mind–one that would sprout three years later.

15
Recovery

The chemotherapy ended and radiation began. For the next 18 days, doctors zapped Jarrett's skull to shrink the tumor. They had drawn marks on the top of his head to pinpoint the targets.

Jarrett's stem cell transplant was really a two-part process. After a 60-day recovery period, the other half of the collected cells would be returned to the boy's body.

"The doctors had a 'keep it coming' attitude," his mother said. "They wanted to do everything possible to make sure cancerous cells couldn't survive in his body."

So, they killed off the marrow once again, this time with radiation. Eight times in fours days, Jarrett squeezed his body into a box, standing behind lead-lined shields to protect his lungs and liver as radiation penetrated his body.

Jennifer got another surprise at this time. The doctors told her Jarrett was doing so well that the next stem cell transplant could be done on an out-patient basis.

"They gave me IV bags filled with antibiotics and fluids to take to our apartment," she said. "It was somewhat disconcerting to think I'd now be responsible for his care, but I had been through training for it. It was good to think about spending less time in the hospital."

Around The Hutch, Jarrett's progress was all the buzz. He was a model patient and a perfect example of "everything going right." Someone from the public relations department approached Jennifer about bringing cameras to the apartment. They wanted to make a training video for other parents. For one of the few times in her life, Jennifer said no to a request from Jarrett's medical team.

"I just had too much on my plate," she said. "Doug and Claire had gone back to Kentucky and I was shuttling Jarrett back and forth for blood counts, changing IV bags, trying to fix meals, keep the apartment germ-free and so on and so on. I just didn't feel like being in a video."

Those feelings of a nervous breakdown were coming on again and Jennifer was determined not to crack.

She decided to rent a car. Their only transportation had been a van that made daily trips between the apartment building, the grocery and the hospital.

Jennifer loaded Jarrett into the car, picked up a map and headed out into the countryside, with the skyscrapers of Seattle in the rearview mirror.

"We needed to get away, even if just for two or three hours at a time," she said.

"For the first few days, Jarrett couldn't get out and couldn't get in crowds, so we just became explorers in the front seat of a car. It did wonders for our morale. We took a road trip almost every afternoon."

One day, John Hayes, the hospital volunteer who had greeted the flu-stricken patient at the airport, came and said he wanted to show Jarrett one of his favorite places in Seattle. He drove the boy and his mother to a fishing pier near the Ballard Locks. Jarrett got out of the car and sat on a bench, watching the ships pass from one pool to the next.

"Are you getting hungry?" the volunteer asked, after an hour had passed.

Jarrett shook his head affirmatively. He was not hooked to IV nutrition and he sure didn't want a handful of Cheerios.

"Let's try a place I think you'll like," the friend said. "Maybe you can handle a little *real* food."

And the Mynears were introduced to Chinook's seafood restaurant. As soon as they walked in, the smell of fried batter hit them like a letter from home.

Jarrett had a few bites of fish, three or four French fries and half of a hush puppy.

"That really helped him snap out of his funk," Jennifer said. "Just like that, he was eating solid food again. We made several more trips to Chinook's in the days to come."

During one of the trips, the volunteer made a detour, driving Jarrett north on Aurora Avenue. They crossed a bridge and exited, making right turns until they were underneath the structure. Then Jarrett saw it. The Fremont Troll. It's one of the most popular, and strangest, art pieces in Seattle.

The large sculpture crouches under the bridge. Or, as locals say, it lurks. The Troll has a shiny hubcap for an eye and a long, stony beard. One hand grasps a real Volkswagen Beetle.

Jarrett wanted to get out of the car and get a closer look. He thought it was just about the neatest thing he'd ever seen. He ambled over and looked up into the giant's face, awestruck.

Then more trolls appeared–real people in funny costumes with crooked walking sticks.

"Jarrett, we've been waiting for you," one of the trolls called out.

Other kids may've been scared. But not Jarrett. He was delighted the actors knew his name and went right up to shake their hands and play along with their silly skit.

"Do you like the Troll?" an actor asked.

Jarrett nodded.

"He likes you, too. He thinks you look delicious!"

Jarrett stepped back in mock horror and everybody laughed. In fact, his laughter was constant for nearly an hour as he joked with the actors, tried on their robes and forgot all about his cancer. There was some magic under that bridge, conjured up by the hospital volunteer, courtesy of the Fremont Arts Council.

The family lingered there, gawking, and watching the other people who came by. Some came to take pictures. Others talked to the Troll and seemed to be expecting it to answer. A couple even left flowers, apparently as some kind of good luck ritual.

In the next few days, the Mynears discovered more about this part of the city. Fremont is the arts district, full of quirky shops run by aging hippies and hip new agers. The street corners are home to musicians and mimes, painters and puppeteers. It was a happy place for Jarrett.

And he always asked to go back under the bridge to see the Troll.

Susan Sever directed a school at The Hutch. She and two other teachers tutored children one on one and in small groups. Most of their students were patients. Some were siblings or the sons and daughters of patients.

She wasn't particularly fond of working with kindergartners. She usually tutored the children of middle school age, preferring to teach geography, math and science. She let another woman take care of beginning readers and kids who liked to finger-paint.

But when Jarrett was there, the patient load was out of balance. There weren't many middle schoolers in the hospital, but the high school and grade school teachers were overloaded.

"I decided I could handle one kindergartner," Susan said.

The first time she walked into a hospital room to meet Jarrett, she wondered what she had gotten herself into.

"He was hyper," she said. "He was climbing all over the place and talking 90 miles a minute. When I told him I was there to teach him how to add and subtract numbers, he said, 'I already know that.' So, I said we'd work on the alphabet. And he said he didn't need help with that either. He seemed like a know-it-all."

But Susan soon learned that Jarrett could back up his bragging. She was amazed at how much he already knew. And, like so many others, she was taken aback by his vocabulary.

"For such a tiny guy, he could sure use some huge words," she recalled.

Soon, she fell under Jarrett's spell and found herself spending more time in his room than she ever planned.

"I found out how smart he was and how adorable he was," she said. "It was like we were on the same level, even though he was only five. Everything he said cracked me up. I had been ready to stay on the sidelines and see how quickly I could pass him off to another teacher. But after a couple of weeks, there was no way I was giving up my star pupil."

Susan had a friend whose daughter was about to be married. For a fun assignment, she decided to have Jarrett dictate some guidelines for a good marriage. The "handbook" was turned into a gift.

Jarrett's entries including the following advice:

1. Show you love someone by giving them presents.
2. Tell the other person when they do things you don't like.
3. If the other person starts an argument, tell them to stop.
4. If the other person doesn't stop, leave the room so you don't have to listen anymore.

Dr. Joyce Brothers couldn't have given any better advice.

One day when Jarrett was in a makeshift classroom set up at the hospital, a delivery man came to door with some items for the school.

Jarrett played in the far end of the room as Susan signed for the package.

The delivery man seemed unsettled to be there and asked Susan in a low voice if all the kids there had cancer.

"Not all of them, " she said, as Jarrett got up and bounced over to the doorway. "But this one does. Look at his bald head."

She patted his shiny scalp playfully. The man still looked uncomfortable.

"Actually," Jarrett spoke up ("actually" had become his favorite word), " I've had cancer since I was two. It was in my leg and they cut it off. Now, it's in my skull but they can't cut my head off!"

Then he let out a loud, hysterical laugh.

"That man backed out of the room quickly and *actually* seemed frightened," Susan said.

Jarrett and Susan joked the rest of the day about how it would be if the hospital cut kids' heads off. There'd be little monsters roaming the halls, holding their hats in their hands because they wouldn't know what to do with them. It was silly talk–the kind that keeps your mind off the bad stuff.

Susan's philosophy was that tutoring provides hope.

"School is a future-oriented thing," she said. "If you instill in a child that he needs to learn his multiplication tables, the implication is that he's going to live."

She'd read lesson plans to children as they drew their last breaths because she believed in staying positive until the end.

When Jarrett was five, she honestly didn't think she'd get to spend many more months with him. But since then, she's made annual trips to Kentucky to see her all-time favorite student.

"I've packed my bags many times, thinking I'd have to go back to Lexington for a funeral," she said "Jennifer would tell me that Jarrett had relapsed. I'd brace myself and get really sad. Then, in no time, he would rise again, and be as vibrant and mischievous as ever."

Susan said she hasn't been a "super-spiritual" person, but "there's something special that keeps Jarrett hanging on. His life has a reason."

In 1999, Susan was diagnosed with non-Hodgkin's lymphoma.

She told Jarrett about it on her annual visit to see him.

"He gave me the greatest pep talk and told me how the bone marrow aspiration I was scheduled for wouldn't really hurt that much," she said. "He told me it was OK to be sad but only for a little while. Then he said you have to get on with life."

Spring passed and summer arrived in Seattle. Now, homesickness really took over. Jennifer wanted to tend to her garden back in Kentucky and eat hamburgers fixed on the grill behind their house. She missed bluegrass traditions, such as attending the horse races at the Keeneland track. Jarrett was ready to go back and play outside with his friends and show off his newfound video game skills. That Sega system from The Dream Factory had gotten a workout. Jarrett had reached the highest level of play on every game he owned.

"He used to sit in the clinic and get so excited with those games that his hands and legs would twitch," Jennifer laughed. "One nurse asked if he ever put the thing down. It was his 'clinic thing.' He never touched it at the apartment."

Mother and son set a goal. They hoped to get back to Kentucky in time for Jennifer's birthday, July 11th. She made the airplane reservations.

"The doctors said that wasn't the way things should be handled," Jennifer said. "But they had faith in our doctors in Kentucky and knew that we lived close to a hospital. So they agreed they would try to approve Jarrett's release by our pre-determined return date."

Jennifer began sending things back to Kentucky. They had accumulated so much stuff that it cost $200 in shipping charges. Some things they could leave behind, but not the three toys Jarrett had received from The Pink Ladies. They were good luck charms.

16
Saying Thanks

They got home on their schedule. Jarrett didn't really get to roam the fields and run the ridges like he had hoped.

His parents had to be strict about visitors and going places. They had been told it would take about a year after the transplant for Jarrett's immune system to build back up.

But he was home, in his own room. Best of all, they felt like a family again. Discussions took place across the dinner table, instead of through a phone line.

Jarrett had been home just a couple of weeks when his friends at The Dream Factory came calling again, this time to give him a job.

They wanted him to be their special guest speaker at their annual gala, an elegant affair when many of the region's movers and shakers made big pledges to help pay for "dreams." It was to be a dinner and dance in the ballroom of the Marriott Griffin Gate resort hotel, followed by silent and live auctions.

"We didn't know that meant hundreds of people in the same room," his mother said, admitting naivety. "He was supposed to be in isolation. But he wanted to do it, so we said he could."

Jarrett's appearance was to be a surprise to the people in the audience. The organization's president, Terry DeLuca, kept him out of sight until it was time to begin the program from the podium.

Jennifer and Doug sat at a table near the front of the banquet hall, feeling intimidated and underdressed. The room was full of men in tuxedos and women in beautiful evening gowns. They had scanned the bid sheets on the tables spread with silent auction items and could see money was no object to a lot of these people.

Jennifer wore a nice dress, but it certainly was not a ball gown, and Doug had on a gray suit and tie. They wondered if they really stuck out as badly as they felt they did. And, nervously, they wondered what might come out of Jarrett's mouth when he got behind the microphone.

Their apprehension vanished quickly. When Terry began to

71

introduce Jarrett, she choked up. She told the crowd about Jarrett's ten-dollar donation and how he had been the first child to send money back to the organization that had helped fulfill scores of dreams.

"He's here tonight so you can see where your money goes," she said. "He'd like to speak to all of the donors. Please welcome Jarrett Mynear."

Jarrett strode to the stage, looking sharp in his tiny rented tux and red bow tie.

The crowd rose to its feet in unison and the applause was loud and long. Doug and Jennifer stood too, overwhelmed by the reception their son was receiving.

When the crowd settled down, Jarrett pulled a short and simple speech out of his pants pocket.

"I don't know how to thank you enough," he said. "Your gifts helped me get through a lot of lonely days. Terry asked me if I'd read my letter to you, so here goes..."

He then read from another piece of paper, the thank you note he had sent earlier that year–the one that was wrapped around a ten-dollar bill.

Again, the crowd erupted in approval. Jennifer looked around and saw a lot of people wiping tears from their eyes. Then she realized. These people weren't there because they had big bank accounts. They were there because they had big hearts.

After the speech, Jarrett's parents couldn't keep up with their son.

"He was working the room like a politician," Jennifer said. "Everyone was asking to have a word with him–asking us to send him over to their table next."

He posed for pictures, signed autographs and got his cheeks pinched by well-meaning ladies more than a few times.

As the evening progressed, a band took the stage and the dancing began. The lead singer called Jarrett up to the stage and handed him the microphone. The next thing Doug and Jennifer knew, their son was singing along to the Bob Seger classic, "Old Time Rock and Roll."

There was the squeaky voice amplified. His parents just shook their heads. Apparently Jarrett had been talking to more people than they realized. They didn't know when he'd had a word with the band, but somehow a conversation had won him a solo in the spotlight.

It wasn't exactly beautiful music, but it was as uplifting as any hymn. It was the sound of a happy heart and it filled the room.

17
The Silly Season

Jarrett started first grade in January 1996, once more running about a half term behind everyone else in his class. Again, on his first day, he explained his medical condition to his fellow students. He took a sharpened pencil and stabbed it into his right leg.

Some of the kids gasped.

Jarrett laughed.

"See, it's not real and some of you didn't even know it," he said. "I'm not handicapped."

"The teachers and principal were very sensitive to Jarrett's needs," Jennifer said. "The school let me draw up a letter asking the other parents to please keep their children at home if there were any signs of illness–the flu, chicken pox, mumps or measles. They were all cooperative and understanding."

Jarrett turned seven in April, finished first grade in May and had a summer to remember.

He went swimming almost every day. He played in the woods. He teased his sister. Two or three times a week, one of his adult friends from The Dream Factory or church or the neighborhood took Jarrett out to eat or to a movie or baseball game.

"He had a better social life than we did," Jennifer said. "He was as comfortable in a room full of adults as he was on the playground."

Jarrett was due for a checkup at "The Hutch." The doctors there like to see their patients on an annual basis for a progress report. The family planned its return for mid-June, on purpose. The Fremont Arts Council–all those people who played trolls for Jarrett under the bridge–had invited them to be in the Solstice Parade. The Mynears weren't really sure what they were getting into, but it sounded like fun.

Jarrett's exam at "The Hutch" went off without a hitch. So they stayed in Seattle a few extra days, awaiting the Saturday closest to the first day of summer–parade day.

"The Solstice Parade is unlike anything you've ever seen," Doug said. "There are only two rules for entrants. You can do anything you want as long as it's not in a motorized vehicle. All the floats had to be human-powered. And there could be no advertising."

The arts council reserved a place for the Mynears on a large pull cart made up to look like a pirate's ship. The theme was Peter Pan. Jarrett was given a pirate's costume, complete with a plastic sword and golden necklaces. Claire was dressed up as Tinkerbell. Jennifer decided she'd just walk along beside the float, out of costume. Doug was glad of that. The fewer things on the float, the better.

"I found out I was there to play horse," he said. "They needed me to help pull the thing and it was heavy. There were four other guys there to help, but a couple of them spent more time dancing in the street."

Tens of thousands of people lined the street. It was outrageous— sort of a northwestern Mardi Gras–a way for people in a rainy climate to welcome the season of sunshine. They passed street performers and fire-eaters, drag queens and belly dancers. A gay-themed Wizard of Oz float told them Dorothy wasn't in Kansas anymore. And the Mynears sure weren't in Kentucky.

Jarrett looked like a king, albeit a scruffy one with a fake beard and eye patch, as he waved to the crowds and took in the wonders.

"At one point, a group of bicyclists whisked by us on the street," Doug said. "They were all nude. I looked back at Jennifer and she looked horrified. Then we looked up at Jarrett. He was grinning ear to ear."

"Oh well," Jennifer said later. "What could we do about it? You can't control streakers and it gave Jarrett another good story to tell when he got back home."

18
"Go, Jarrett, Go"

The Dream Factory gala rolled around again and Jarrett wasn't about to miss it. His parents tried to tell him it was an adult affair and his invitation last year had been an exception.

"Remember," his mother said, "you were the only kid in the room."

But deep down Jarrett believed he'd be invited back. He loved The Dream Factory and he had sent the organization another ten dollars in the past year. Didn't all donors get an invitation?

He was right, of course. When Doug and Jennifer's invitation arrived in the mail, the handwritten addition was clear: *"Please bring Jarrett. We look forward to seeing him again."*

Jarrett was especially interested in the silent auction. The year before he had paid close attention to all the items spread out on tables awaiting the highest bidders–neat things such as computer scanners, cell phones, boom boxes and calculators. He'd like to try his hand at naming his own price for some neat gadgets.

Granny Mynear had given him $40 just for that purpose. It nearly burned a hole in his pocket. As soon as they arrived, he began to peruse the treasures up for bid.

Just like the year before, Doug and Jennifer soon found themselves on the edge of the room watching Jarrett get the star treatment. Again, he was doing the shake-and-howdy "nice to meet you" routine.

At one point, they saw their son sitting on top of a Sea-Doo personal watercraft that was to be auctioned off. Moments later, they scanned the room again and saw him in the driver's seat of a go-cart, brightly painted with Valvoline Oil logos and slogans.

His name was the first one to be written on the bid sheet for the go-cart. He'd gladly spend the whole forty for the shiny machine.

"He was having the time of his life," Jennifer said. "After we'd been there awhile, someone came over and asked, 'Do you know who Jarrett's talking to now?'"

They didn't recognize the handsome gentleman who was showing

Jarrett around the auction items.

"That's Ron Turner," they were told. "He's one of the most successful businessmen here."

Turner was a developer and the chief operating officer of Amteck, an electrical contracting company that did business all over the world. He had invested wisely and his home was one of the city's showiest. Each Christmas, he and his wife Linda covered their all-white mansion with thousands of miniature lights and invited sick and underprivileged children in to see Santa Claus. Ron put on the beard and took each child on his lap to hear their wishes.

To Jarrett, he was just another nice guy in the room–someone he was glad to get to know.

An hour before the bidding was to end on the silent auction, while Jarrett was still shaking hands and posing for pictures, board member Ralph Coldiron came over to the table to whisper something to Doug and Jennifer.

"Mr. Turner wants to know if it's OK for him to buy the go-cart for Jarrett," Coldiron said.

"We were astounded," Jennifer said. "What were we supposed to say? If we said 'no,' it would look like we were being mean. We knew the money would go to The Dream Factory, which was a great thing. Ralph said Mr. Turner sincerely wanted to give it to Jarrett. In fact, he was already working behind the scenes, encouraging other potential buyers to make sure he got the last bid."

"I could tell by watching Jarrett that he really wanted it," Ron said later. "I really didn't care how high the bidding got."

The clock approached 11 p.m., way past Jarrett's bedtime. But Doug and Jennifer let him stay to see how the auction would turn out.

The emcee began a countdown to officially close the bidding.

"Three... two... one... all done."

The last bid on the clipboard next to the go-cart was by Ron Turner for $900–more than three times what it was worth. But he had purposely placed the bid out of reach.

Everyone still in the room knew Ron didn't plan to ride around in the thing and they watched as he made his way over to Jarrett's table.

"Congratulations, Jarrett," he said, extending his hand. "Looks like you get the go-cart."

"That's not possible," Jarrett said. "I only bid $40. I know it went for a lot more than that."

"The best bid wins," Ron said. "Your bid wasn't the highest one, but it was the best one."

Jarrett was overjoyed and couldn't find the words to thank Mr. Turner enough. All the way home that night he was thinking about that colorful go-cart. Gala organizers had promised to deliver it the next day. Jarrett would be waiting at the crack of dawn.

The next morning, a van pulled into the driveway at the Mynear's home. Jarrett heard the noise and ran to the window. He saw two men unloading his dream machine.

Jarrett rushed out and claimed his prize, eager to take it for a test drive. But that would have to wait. The car needed some modifications. Ron had thought of that, too. He had sent word that he'd be out to measure little Jarrett and check out the position of the controls, the gas pedals and the brake.

For two days, Jarrett spent several hours just sitting in the cart, making racecar noises with his mouth and whipping the steering wheel right and left. At last, on the third day after the auction, Ron showed up with his two sons, took Jarrett's measurements and loaded the go-cart into a pickup truck.

"Don't worry," he told Jarrett. "We'll bring it back in a couple days."

Over the years, Ron and Linda Turner got to know the Mynears quite well. They always invited the family to their Christmas party, as well as company picnics at Amteck. The Turners often invited Jarrett out to eat at some of his favorite restaurants because they loved to hear him talk about life.

"You never heard about his problems," Ron said. "He never complained about anything. He fueled my heart. He had more hope than anyone I knew and no fear. Being with him was like being in church. It made me thank God for how fortunate I was. I needed him around to help me keep my focus on what was important. A visit with the Pope couldn't have had more impact on me."

When the go-cart came back, it was custom-fit for Jarrett. His name was painted on the side right where the driver would sit. And Claire's name decorated the back panel. She was listed as "Pit Crew."

Jarrett got in, started up the engine, let his foot off the brake and headed off through the yard.

"Watch out for the bushes!" his mom called out.

Jarrett swerved a little to the right, then a little to the left, and eventually got the thing straightened out. Jennifer thought her son was going to give her a heart attack with this new "toy." But, she remembered all the months when Jarrett's mode of transportation had been a wheelchair or a gurney–when his daily route was from a hospital room to an examining table.

"Go, Jarrett, go!" she yelled, hugging Doug and laughing as their little Mario Andretti did donuts in the back yard.

19
After Summer Comes the Fall

Jarrett started second grade in the fall, and all signs were that he was bouncing back from his cancer just fine.

Then September came. The Mynears had come to dread the ninth month of the year. It was at a September football game when Jarrett first alerted his family to his "hurts" as a toddler. And it was September of his kindergarten year when he was diagnosed for the second time with Ewing's sarcoma.

As the calendar turned again, so did their luck. Jennifer discovered another lump on Jarrett's head.

"He kept telling us he bumped his head on the swing set," she said. "But the bruise on his head wasn't in the same spot as the bump."

Jarrett seemed to be searching for any explanation he could find. He didn't want to believe it could be cancer again. Neither did his parents.

"Mom, I'm sure it's where the swing hit me," he insisted. "You worry too much."

But the lump was quite visible, the size of a pea. It doubled in size overnight as he slept. And that was that. There would be no arguments or second-guessing. His mother took him straight to the hospital.

The doctors performed a fine needle aspirate, which means they sucked cells from the lump through a hollow needle. The results showed the cells were cancerous.

Again, the calls and consultations began between the doctors at UK, the Mayo Clinic and "The Hutch."

The bottom line was the stem cell transplant had not worked, at least not permanently. Although it had seemed to build Jarrett's strength and keep the cancer at bay for a while, it had not killed off every trace of the disease.

The doctors suggested yet another round of chemotherapy.

Doug and Jennifer were told that Ewing's sarcoma was considered to be a "smart cancer." The disease learns to adapt to chemotherapy. Treatment that works for a while can soon become ineffective. It's sort of like the flu. The vaccines are ever-changing as new strains turn up and the body adapts to the shots. Or think of cockroaches. You can spray a house with pesticides and get rid of the bugs for a while. But over time, they can become resistant to the chemicals and can thrive despite your efforts to kill them. You have to find different, stronger sprays. The "cancer bugs" in Jarrett's system just hadn't been exterminated.

"We now knew Ewing's was just not going to go away for good," Jennifer said.

So, the next round of chemo was different than all the previous ones. The doctors tried new combinations of pills and poisons. Jarrett was pulled out of school and Jennifer officially resigned from teaching.

By this time, the Mynears had another situation to complicate their lives. Claire had been diagnosed with ADHD, Attention-Deficit Hyperactivity Disorder. She also suffered from sensory motor integration dysfunction. From about the time she was three, they noticed she had trouble following instructions. And her speech was slurred.

Although her body was healthy, her mind was not developing as it should. She had all the symptoms you associate with a "hyper" child–a short attention span, bursts of high energy and a low tolerance for frustration. She could be an extremely loving, outgoing child one minute and shy and reclusive the next.

Her parents were determined to help her get the disorders under control. That meant another child with appointments to make, medicine to take and obstacles to shake, as they shuttled her to meetings with occupational and speech therapists.

This family was burning the candle at both ends and in the middle. To borrow another cliche, at times they truly didn't know which end was up.

The routine continued through the fall and winter. By summer, the Mynears had taken on a whole new attitude about Jarrett's lot in life.

"We had let the cancer rule our lives long enough," Jennifer said.

"During each round of treatment before, we kept a tight rein on him. We decided to stop being so protective and isolating of Jarrett. If someone wanted to take him somewhere, within reason, we let him go. If visitors wanted to come by, we made them feel welcome."

They took advantage of every opportunity to go swimming and hiking. They made many trips to Nicholas County, so Jarrett could trek in the woods around Granny and Paw Mynear's farm. And they also decided that summer to send Jarrett to camp.

It was a decision they'd never regret.

20
Indian Summer Camp

Many people had tried to sell the Mynears on the idea of sending their son to camp. Parents of other children with cancer, doctors, nurses, and friends from the American Cancer Society all told them how uplifting the experience could be. Kids could go at the age of seven, but they didn't think Jarrett was strong enough for it then.

But during the summer of his eighth year–the summer they decided to let Jarrett live life to its fullest–they let him sign up for Indian Summer Camp. Jarrett had seen the brochures and was more than ready for a week of "roughing it."

Doug and Jennifer drove their son to the camp, an hour away in Estill County. The last three miles of the journey were down a narrow, gravel road, where tree branches formed a tunnel and kudzu vines dropped down from utility poles. They wondered if they were taking their son into a wilderness full of spiders, snakes, poisonous plants and swollen streams. Jarrett hoped so. He envisioned himself as an Indiana Jones sort of adventurer, as he pressed his nose to the car window and waited for a glimpse of his weeklong home away from home.

"It would be the longest he'd ever been away from us," Jennifer said. "We were worried, but yet we knew many of the doctors and nurses who would be there to take care of him. They were ones he'd already worked with. We trusted them, so we had to learn to let go a little."

They felt better when the road opened up into a clearing and they got their first glimpse of the campsite. The first thing Jarrett saw was the swimming pool. He'd be in that thing first chance he got.

There were rows of cabins and a large central building. They saw a volleyball net, a pit for campfires and a lake lined with canoes. The lawns were neatly mowed and the sun dropped light on the miniature village, making it look like an oasis in the middle of nowhere.

And, for Jarrett, the best sight of all was other kids–dozens of them, laughing and running around like they didn't have a care in the world. Many of them were bald, some were missing limbs and a couple were in wheelchairs. But if you closed your eyes and listened to their laughter and their chatter, you could've been at any camp in the country. Sure, this was "cancer camp," but it was about living, not about coddling kids and concentrating on their troubles. There would be no pep talks or speeches about coping with the disease. As much as possible, the camp's counselors aimed to ignore individual disabilities. Everyone here was in the same boat and, for this week, that boat was pulling up anchor and setting sail.

Jennifer and Doug met the counselors, chatted with some of the other parents and took a good look around. With dusk approaching, they headed back up the gravel road in their car, telling themselves and each other that Jarrett would be just fine. It had been good to see all those kids they'd come to know in hospitals at someplace more pleasant.

"But truthfully, we worried every night," Jennifer said. "This was before cell phones were prevalent. I'd worry when I left the house to run an errand or go to the store that someone from the camp would be trying to reach us. I gave them about 20 phone numbers."

The camp director called the Mynears midway through the week. When the phone rang, Jennifer immediately feared something was wrong.

But the director was calling only to check in and tell them Jarrett was having a wonderful time.

"She told us that even though Jarrett was one of the youngest kids there, he had become somewhat of a leader," Jennifer said. "She said Jarrett was the voice of reason when some of the other kids wanted to get into things beyond their abilities."

And she said the young man was willing to try any activity the counselors had planned. He excelled at the arts and crafts; he was among the first to volunteer for any game and some of the girls appeared to have a crush on him. That made Jennifer smile. She could picture her talkative son getting tongue-tied around the young ladies. And she knew he'd be trying to hide in a corner on the last night of camp when a dance was on the agenda.

The counselors were especially happy that Jarrett had tackled a 30-foot climbing wall. As he pulled himself to the top, his prosthesis came unattached and tumbled to the ground.

"Oospy," Jarrett shouted. "Look out below!"

Everyone laughed.

People often brag that they can beat their competitors with one arm tied behind their back. Jarrett could do it with one leg lying on the ground.

The week went quickly for Jarrett.

"I had a blast," he said. "I was the only kid there with Ewing's, I think. But I really didn't know what the other kids had. We didn't talk about it. That was one of the nicest things about it. No one felt sorry for us."

Every day, even though it rained a lot, the campers went to the pool. Swimming was Jarrett's favorite pastime. To visitors, the pool deck could be an unsettling sight at first. The chain link fence was lined with artificial limbs, as the kids bobbed around in the water unhindered by manmade devices. Some of the kids wore caps, to keep from getting sunburned on the top of their bald heads.

What else did the kids do? Anything you can name as a camp activity probably occurred there. They made beaded necklaces and tie-dyed T-shirts. They played hide and seek in the woods, fished in a pond and played "horse" on the basketball court. They took up archery and practiced self-defense. And at night, they sang songs around the campfire and told ghost stories after the lights went out.

For Jarrett, the last day was the best of all. It was a day when his skill at video games would serve him well in a real life battle–a battle of precision and wits where no one got hurt. The campers had been told they could end the week with "the water fight to end all water fights." And they came armed with their super-soakers.

The campers formed a circle in an open field, holding their weapons, with their hearts racing. They had teased each other all week.

"Wait 'til the water fight. You're the first one I'm going to soak."

"That's what you think. I'll get you first."

"The wetter the better. Bring it on!"

When the director gave the signal, the fury began. With squeals of delight, the campers ran around for more than an hour, soaking each other from top to bottom. The counselors got in on it too and the kids ganged up on them.

"Some firefighters were there with one of their trucks," Jarrett recalled. "They had a big hose we could use to refill our guns. And they let the kids take turns using the hose to shoot streams of water into the crowd."

There were no winners in the battle. Everyone was equally drenched and equally delighted. It looked as if that same boat they were all in had capsized. But everyone came up gasping for air. Actually, they were breathing in life, deeply, and drinking in all that was good about childhood.

In later years, the water fights ceased. The camp moved to a new location and new operators decided to ban anything that resembled weapons or warfare. Most of the parents thought it was a shame. On one hand they could understand the argument. But the kids missed the battles and no one saw them as violent or aggressive. It was good, clean fun and by the end of the week, the campers needed cleansing.

"I think that first week, Jarrett had had one bath," Jennifer laughed. "He came back with rashes and lots of dirt under his nails and behind the ears. The water battle had made a muddy field even messier. The counselors just kind of went with the flow."

Their son, who had spent much of his life in pristine hospital rooms and apartments sterilized with Clorox, had been allowed to get down and dirty. It seemed right. He had wrestled germs and handled worms. In other words, he was allowed to be a normal eight-year-old boy.

Jarrett never missed camp after that.

"Going back the next year was an automatic," his mother said.

Several of his counselors kept in touch with him throughout the years and his doctors were good about working his chemotherapy schedules around camp.

Once patients turn 18, they can no longer attend Indian Summer Camp unless they come back as counselors. Jarrett decided the first year to make that a goal.

"I plan to keep going there as long as I live," Jarrett said. "It's been one of the highlights of my life and if I can give back by being a counselor, I'll definitely do it."

Now, he even dances with the girls.

21
Promotion

Jarrett attended third grade for two weeks. And for once, September didn't bring bad news.

"His teacher came to us and said our goals for Jarrett were being squashed," his mother said.

"What do you mean?"

"I mean he's so far ahead of the other kids, he's not getting the social interaction you want him to get in school," the teacher said. "We have him working in a corner on other projects that are more at his level. He's working by himself too much."

The teacher and the principal wanted the Mynears to consider letting Jarrett skip ahead to the fourth grade.

"That shocked us," Doug said. "We knew Jarrett was smart for his age, but he had been out of formal schooling so much that we really didn't think he was that advanced."

His parents were also concerned about his size.

"He was so much smaller than the other kids and this would put him in middle school early," Jennifer said. "We really had to think about it.

"We worried about the maturity factor, but the teacher assured us that wouldn't be a problem. Jarrett had always made friends easily and already knew a lot of the kids in the fourth grade so that wasn't a big issue."

They certainly didn't want to hold Jarrett back and they could tell he was bored with his homework assignments. So they let him move up a grade.

"It was the right thing to do," his mother realized later. "It gave him a sense of belonging."

Jarrett loved going to school. For him, it was a privilege.

"He thought other kids took it for granted and that bothered him," Jennifer said. "When he was out for a chemo treatment or because a flu bug was going around, other kids would say to him that they wished they could stay out of school for a week at a time."

Jarrett bristled at that.

87

"He'd say 'No, you don't know what you're saying. Given the choice between school and chemo, I'll take school any day.'"

Fourth grade was Jarrett's first complete year of elementary school. He was there on the first day and he was there on the last day. He took part in a full cycle of lessons and a full cycle of extracurricular activities, from fall festivals to spring field trips.

But shortly after he turned nine in April, Jennifer's maternal antennas went up again.

"I started seeing symptoms of exhaustion," she said. "He really seemed to be tired and draggy. It was all he could do to get through the day. He'd come home from school and just collapse on the couch. It was not like him at all."

He was still going in for blood counts, which always hovered just above the transfusion level. His platelet count was low and he bled easily.

She talked to his doctors about what was happening and they agreed his blood cell counts should've been building up more by that time.

"They said his marrow was tired. It was just taking him longer to regroup this time around after his latest chemo treatments. They said I needed to relax and be patient. He'd bounce back."

But Jennifer's instincts told her it was something more. Jarrett was developing spider veins on his shoulders and back. That just couldn't be normal, she told herself.

She was right.

22
An Open Book

This is the part of Jarrett's life story that Jennifer had trouble sharing with anyone. It was weird. Mystical even. She was afraid it made her sound crazy.

She was cleaning the house one day and noticed one of their reference books on the shelf–one of the many medical manuals they had acquired over the years. She took the book down and dropped it on the floor.

"I did that just to remind myself to check it out later, after I was finished with the housework," she said. "I thought with it lying out, I'd have to stumble over it and force myself to do a little research."

She did indeed stumble onto something.

When she came back to the book, it was lying open to a page that described a condition called myelodysplasia.

"I had never heard of it before," she said, "but I was immediately drawn to the article."

The symptoms it described matched what she was seeing in Jarrett–lethargy, spider veins and low blood counts. The disease was defined as a pre-leukemia condition that develops when the bone marrow wears out. It was typically a disease of elderly people.

"I had the strangest feeling that I was supposed to see that article," Jennifer said. "It was like a guardian angel led me to it. I thought maybe even my dead father had a hand in it.

"I know that sounds loony, but that's how I felt."

She asked Jarrett's doctors if he could have developed myelodysplasia. They said it was a possibility, but a remote one.

Doug had to leave for business on a Monday morning, the same day as Jarrett's next doctor's appointment. His company assigned him to Italy to work on a reverse osmosis water treatment plant at a U.S. naval base. It was just the second time his employer had sent him overseas.

Jennifer dropped her husband off at the airport on her way to taking Jarrett to the doctor's office. He kissed his wife, son and daughter goodbye, promising to return in a week with some souvenirs from Naples.

At the clinic, Jennifer again asked about the article she'd read.

"They were respectful of my instincts and said they'd do a bone marrow biopsy to test for a blood virus or something that could be causing the low counts. They thought a biopsy would rule out myelodysplasia."

Once again, they stuck a large needle in Jarrett's hip and drew out marrow. Then mother and son went home to wait for the results.

Doug called as soon as he got settled into his hotel room in Naples, just to let his family know he had arrived safely and to give out the phone numbers where he could be reached. There was a six-hour time difference. It was late at night in Italy, but still early evening in Kentucky.

"I told him about the bone marrow biopsy," Jennifer said. "I could hear concern in his voice. He tends to be more optimistic than me and he hadn't really thought the doctors would see a need to do more tests."

"Let me know the minute you hear anything," Doug said. "I won't be able to sleep until I know something."

As soon as Jennifer hung up from talking to Doug, the phone rang again. It was Jarrett's doctor. Bad news traveled through the telephone line like a bolt of lightning. If anyone else had been in the room, they'd have seen Jennifer's complexion turn instantly pale, her posture slump, and they'd have heard her voice become a quivering whisper.

The voice on the other end confirmed her fears. Jarrett did indeed have myelodysplasia. His bloodstream contained leukemia cells–the result of all the chemotherapy that had ravaged his body over the past seven years. Now Jarrett was battling two diseases.

"What do we do now?" she managed to ask the doctor, as she felt her knees go weak.

He said there were really only two options. The first was palliative care, which basically means just doing your best to make the patient comfortable until the disease takes over. The other was a bone marrow transplant.

The message was loud and clear. Jarrett was at death's door. The doctor didn't put it in those words, but that was understood.

The diagnosis came on the eighth anniversary of the death of

Jennifer's father.

"I couldn't have felt sadder," she said. "I was truly almost ready to give up, sort of thinking enough was enough. I didn't want to face my son again, who was feeling miserable, and tell him he had another disease and needed another risky treatment."

She told herself that maybe it was selfish to try to keep him alive. She loved him more than words could tell, but was it fair to put him through so much? If God wanted Jarrett so badly, maybe they should let Him have him. The thoughts swirled through her mind and she'd get mad at herself for even thinking of giving up. Then, she'd get mad when she thought her decision might prolong Jarrett's pain. She needed Doug to help her think it through.

She tried to call his hotel room, but she couldn't get an operator who spoke English. She didn't know anyone who spoke Italian who could put in a call for her. She tried several times, but each time she hit a brick language barrier. So Jennifer sat by the phone, knowing Doug would call her as soon as he could.

On the other side of the Atlantic Ocean, Doug too had trouble getting an operator who could help him make a connection. After several frustrating attempts, he went to bed. He tossed and turned and stared at the clock.

The next morning, he went ahead to work. It was 8 a.m. in Naples but just 2 a.m. in Kentucky. He didn't want to disturb his family in the middle of their night. And he assumed Jennifer hadn't heard back from the hospital yet.

Late that afternoon, Naples-time, Doug did get to a phone and got through to his wife. When he got the news, his reaction was the same as Jennifer's. He too turned pale and weak, feeling as if he'd been run over by a steamroller.

"I immediately said I had to get home," Doug said. "There were two other guys from the company on the trip. They could take over my part of the presentation."

He told Jennifer he'd be on the first flight he could get out of Naples. The company would help him make the arrangements.

But before he hung up, he left Jennifer with some words that helped her put things in focus.

"We've been through all these years together and not once has Jarrett shown any signs of being a quitter," Doug told his wife.

"He'll be the one to tell us when it's time to give up. We'll have a long, honest talk with him and see what *he* wants to do."

They were both pretty sure they knew what Jarrett's answer would be.

23
A Perfect Match

To even consider a transplant, doctors would have to find a donor—someone whose bone marrow matched Jarrett's tissue type.

Bone marrow is a soft fatty tissue that produces blood cells. Marrow damaged by chemotherapy and radiation can't produce enough white cells to fight infection.

The doctors told Jennifer that parents rarely provide a marrow match for a child. Brothers and sisters match somewhat more often, but it's usually a stranger who provides the marrow for a transplant. Still, they wanted Jennifer and Claire to be tested right away. Doug would be tested as soon as he returned from Italy.

There are several stages of testing. Jennifer did not match even in the first stage. Claire did.

"Claire was physically drawn into this," Jennifer said. "That worried us. Doug and I would've gladly given anything—arms, legs, organs. But we didn't know if Claire could handle it."

Doug got in late Thursday, weary from travel. He went through the blood testing the next morning and he wasn't a match either. But more good news came back concerning Claire. Every stage of the testing showed her to be a perfect match. Doctors called it the best case scenario. The Mynears weren't so sure about that.

"We were concerned about the emotional trauma for her, not just the physical trauma," Jennifer said. She hadn't liked it at all when they drew blood for the tests and her hyperactivity was still a concern. Although she'd grown up in and around hospitals, she'd never been a patient.

That night at home, Doug and Jennifer had that long, honest talk with Jarrett. They told their nine-year-old son just what they knew about myelodysplasia. They told him it was the reason he felt tired all the time, why he bruised easily and why he sometimes bled without any reason. They told him it could develop into leukemia, a full-blown blood disease.

"We tried to remind him what a transplant meant," Jennifer said. "It meant intensive chemotherapy, a long hospital stay and months of recovery. We asked him if he was up for it."

"I don't have much of a choice," Jarrett said emphatically. "It's either do it or lie down and die and I'm not going to lie down and die."

His parents looked at each other knowingly. It was the answer they had expected–certainly, the one they wanted.

Next, Doug and Jennifer went to Claire and tried to explain to her what was ahead. Jarrett too had expressed concern about drawing his little sister into the process.

But Jennifer sensed something as she talked to Claire. The girl seemed to take pride in the fact that she was the only one in the family who could help Jarrett now. During all those previous trips to hospitals, she had been helpless to do anything for her big brother. In all her hyperactivity over the years, she always seemed to understand that she had to take it easy around Jarrett. She couldn't jump on him or play too roughly with him. When he needed his sleep, she knew to tiptoe around him. She never seemed jealous of all the attention he got. But now the attention was on her. She could literally save her brother's life.

She told her parents earnestly and lovingly that she'd let the doctors stick needles in her if it would help Jarrett.

"I'll do whatever they need me to do," Claire said. Her parents couldn't have known she'd take it this well. Did she really understand? She was just six years old. They believed she knew enough to know they wouldn't ask her to do it if it wasn't important. They hugged her and told her how special she was.

The next battle was with the insurance company. Bone marrow transplants aren't always covered. Each individual case is considered separately. The company had already paid more than $700,000 for Jarrett's care over the years. It didn't approve new procedures without a lot of scrutiny. This transplant could cost anywhere from $200,000 to $400,000.

"We didn't have time for them to drag their feet," Jennifer said. "Leukemia cells called blasts were developing in his bloodstream and the numbers were increasing each week while we were waiting to see if insurance would pay."

His blast level hovered around 12 to 14 percent. The Mynears were told if it reached 21 percent, the doctors wouldn't do a transplant. It would be too late then. Leukemia would win out.

The Mynears had to decide where to go should the transplant be approved. Usually, a patient would go back to where he or she had their original treatments. But the family was reluctant to pack up and relocate to Seattle again.

Dr. Greg Hale, a pediatric oncologist at UK's Markey Cancer Center, helped the Mynears with their decision.

"He personally delivered research articles to us at our house," Jennifer said. "He'd talk with us over coffee about the procedure and answer any questions we had. He said he had the equipment at Markey to do the transplant. He had done the procedure for patients with myelodysplasia and he was willing to do it again."

They asked Jarrett what he thought.

"These doctors know me here," he said. "They care about me and know what I need. I'd like to stay here close to my family and friends."

"Although Jarrett liked Seattle, he also equated it with the worst time of his life," Doug said. "He didn't want to go there again unless it was to be for a vacation."

That settled it. Once the insurance company said OK, the transplant was scheduled for mid-August at the Markey Cancer Center in Lexington.

By the time the procedure was approved, Jarrett's blast level had reached 17 percent. Once again Jarrett had raced the clock and come in under the wire.

Transplant day came August 12, 1998. Granny Jeanne stayed in Jarrett's room. Doug and Jennifer went into pre-op with Claire. When Dr. Hale was ready, Claire was wheeled into the operating room, with her Sesame Street slippers peeking out from under the sheet. The only smile in the group came from the Muppet character Elmo at the ends of each of her feet.

The doctors gave her an anesthetic and, in a matter of minutes, she fell into a deep sleep. The surgeons bored into Claire's pelvis in two places, using hollow needles to suck the marrow from her bones.

Fluid was drawn from her body into a plastic container. It was then taken away to be filtered and treated.

In a room down the hall, Jarrett was eating tacos and watching television. His immune system was at zero. The marrow in his bones had been completely killed. But the casual observer wouldn't have known he was at a crossroads in his life. He seemed at peace, without a care in the world.

Late in the afternoon, the doctors came into his room. They had the IV bags, which were like presents from his sister. They contained the gift of life.

The tubes were connected to Jarrett's catheter and the fluid began to flow into his body. It was naturally transported back into the bone cavities where it was expected to grow quickly to replace the old bone marrow.

Claire woke up and tried to roll over. A sharp pain shot through her back. She was wrapped around the waist with a large pressure bandage. There was an intravenous needle stuck in her hand, the IV pump was churning–all things she had seen Jarrett experience. She began to cry.

"Honey," her mother said. "It's over. You'll be all right. Jarrett has some of your bone marrow now. We're so proud of you."

Claire slept peacefully through the night and was eager to go home first thing the next morning. She left the cancer center by skipping out the front door, with no need for pain killers. The Mynears realized they had more than one resilient child.

24
Jarrett Gets an Idea

As Jarrett recovered from his bone marrow transplant, he spent another 38 days in isolation at the Markey Cancer Center. But his hospital room looked like a playhouse.

Get well cards covered two walls from ceiling to floor. His mother had brought tacky putty to hang them all where Jarrett could see them. He enjoyed looking at the "wall of love," with its funny pictures, jokes and notes of encouragement.

A friend also supplied their son with a laptop computer, so he could get e-mail and play online games. And one corner of the room was piled high with stuffed animals, books, plastic trucks and puzzles. The Nintendo 64 system seldom sat silent.

Jarrett couldn't leave the room, but plenty of people came to him. It seemed as if the stream of visitors was non-stop–relatives, neighbors, friends and parents of other children who were patients in the hospital. And there were several doctors, nurses and hospital aides who counted themselves among Jarrett's newfound friends. They too popped into the room whenever possible. It was good to see a cheerful child who made them laugh.

The phone rang several times an hour with people wanting to let Jarrett know they were thinking about him.

"It was amazing," Jennifer said. "It really kept him going."

Kathy Tabb, a volunteer with the American Cancer Society who had come to know Jennifer through support groups, became a daily visitor to Jarrett's room.

"We bonded," Kathy said. "I just wanted to relieve some of the strain on Jennifer, but I didn't know what I'd talk to a kid about. But when he found out I was a survivor of ovarian cancer, he just started talking about things that were familiar to me–doctors we both knew, articles we had read, things we did to pass time in the hospital. It was like talking to someone my own age."

Kathy brought daily gifts to Jarrett–mostly junk items she picked up at a dollar store. She always wrapped them and kept him guessing what would come next.

He liked to blow bubbles and squirt water pistols. She gave him lots of things to foster his mischievousness.

"Once I took him a can of silly string and he sprayed it all over his bald head," she said. "He always had the nurses in stitches."

One day, during a rare moment without visitors or phone calls, Jennifer talked to Jarrett about how fortunate he was to have so many people who loved him and wanted to be near him.

"Jarrett had noticed that the rest of the ward seemed quiet compared to his room," said Jennifer. "We talked about the fact that some of the kids didn't have a lot of visitors and didn't get many cards and gifts."

Jennifer stepped out of the room for a few minutes to get a cup of coffee. And in those moments of solitude, Jarrett's mind went to work.

"I thought somebody should do something for those other kids," Jarrett said.

And even though he was just nine years old, Jarrett decided he should be that somebody.

When his mother came back into the room, Jarrett sat up in bed and told her he had an idea. He reminded her about "The Pink Ladies" in Seattle and how much he enjoyed the gifts they brought around once a week. And he mentioned the trinkets Kathy brought him each day.

"Couldn't we get some toys together and start a cart here?" he asked, with such sincerity it almost made his mother cry.

"I was blown away that he came up with that idea," Jennifer said. "He had four catheters hanging out of his chest and was under heavy medication. He was in bad shape and he was thinking of someone else."

Jennifer is the first to admit her son was not always the angel he appeared to be. He could be temperamental and hardheaded, like all pre-teens. But at that moment, she could almost see a halo over his head.

"After the initial shock of him coming up with that suggestion considering the shape he was in, I told him we'd talk to his dad about it," she said.

"I certainly didn't want to discourage it, but I wasn't sure how much thought he'd given it."

Because of their experiences with The Dream Factory, Jennifer knew they had contacts who would probably help them get a gift-giving drive together.

"I thought we might get enough toys to go around the hospital once or twice and then Jarrett would probably lose interest," she said.

"The children's hospital has 50 beds, so I told Jarrett we'd need 50 toys. He had a couple of duplicate toys he said he'd be willing to give away but he didn't want to give out anything that had been used or opened. He wanted the kids to have new toys, not hand-me-downs. That was hospital policy, anyway."

In the weeks that followed, Jarrett was released from the cancer center but he wasn't able to go to school. Doctors feared he'd pick up some childhood disease from such close contact with large numbers of children. Even a common cold could be a setback in all the progress he was making.

A teacher came to the house for two hours a week for homebound lessons, but that wasn't nearly enough instruction time to be acceptable to Jarrett's parents. Jennifer, with her background in teaching, insisted on spending many hours with her son in educational pursuits.

One of those pursuits became the toy cart. Jarrett talked about it all the time. He wanted to make it happen as soon as possible; so his mother told him to work out a business plan.

Jarrett wrote a list of goals and objectives. It was much more ambitious than what his mother had in mind. It soon became obvious Jarrett wanted the toy cart to be a permanent fixture at the hospital, not just something that came around once a year like Christmas.

He wrote letters to the administrators at the hospital seeking their blessing. Then he made a list of people and businesses that might donate. And he went straight to the top, writing letters to the big department store chains such as Toys R Us, Wal-Mart and K-Mart. In fact, every store in Lexington's largest mall got a request for money, toys, or both. Jarrett sent about a hundred letters in all.

Even though the basic request was a form letter, Jarrett signed a personal note attached to each mailing.

Word spread among the family's many friends. Ralph Coldiron, The Dream Factory's past president, was also on the board of the children's hospital. He was instrumental in making sure all the movers and shakers he knew would help make Jarrett's endeavor a reality.

"I saw Jarrett one day in the hall of the clinic," Ralph recalled. "He had a mask on his face and wasn't looking too well. The first thing he said to me was, 'Ralph, I want to start a business. Will you help me?'"

Ralph heard Jarrett's idea and loved it. He told his young friend he'd contact the head of the Children's Hospital Fund to get the ball rolling.

"He was a ball of fire. He knew exactly what he wanted to do."

But admittedly, Ralph didn't act on it right away.

"About a week later, Jennifer called me to ask about it. I asked her how serious Jarrett was and she said it was all he was talking about. I got on it that same day."

Kathy Tabb remembers the first time Jarrett told her about it.

"He said he didn't want a lot of adults getting involved because they'd just have a lot of meetings and waste a lot of time," she said. "That cracked me up. Did he have the business world figured out or what? I've used that quote many times."

The young man also decided to put a little twist on the name of his project. He changed the name from "toy cart" to "joy cart." He said it was about spreading happiness.

"He totally came up with the name," his mother said. "We had to admit 'Jarrett's Joy Cart' had a nice ring to it."

His family decided to keep the items small. They asked for the toys to be valued at no more than ten dollars. They thought it would be easier to stock the cart that way and prevent one child from getting a video game console while another got a box of crayons. Uneven giving might defeat the purpose of spreading joy and harmony.

"Everyone has things they donate to and I thought we might have to dig into our own pockets to make this thing happen," Jennifer said. "I didn't want to disappoint Jarrett if it didn't work."

That was wasted worry. In just a week after the letters went out, Jarrett started getting positive replies and, even better, checks. From the initial mailing, he got a 28 percent response rate. Marketing experts will tell you you're doing well if you get five percent.

The folks at the children's hospital were caught up in the

excitement too. Once the public relations staff found out The Joy Cart had enough donations to make an initial run, it set up a news conference.

"I kept wanting to put it off," Jennifer said, still not sure if the donors were committed long-term. "But once the date was set, there was no stalling."

March 23, 1999 fell during the middle of the NCAA basketball tournament, so local news crews were spread thin. The Mynears were told not to expect a large turnout at the news conference. But the public relations department had received a few phone calls and knew the cart would receive some coverage.

"When we walked into that room, I was amazed," Jennifer said. "There was a room full of reporters and four or five video cameras."

Nearly a dozen microphones cluttered the table, bearing the logos of all the local television affiliates–Fox, ABC, CBS and NBC– and several radio stations. Bright lights were set up in each corner of the room and every other person seated there had a notebook or tape recorder in his or her lap.

"Jarrett had been interviewed one-on-one before to help promote The Dream Factory," Jennifer said. "But he had never faced a barrage like this."

A hospital spokeswoman made a couple of remarks to start the news conference, then turned things over to Jarrett. The nine-year-old calmly outlined how he got the idea for the cart, who donated and how it would work. Then he took questions, expertly describing his cancer and the operations he had been through. He had the audience in the palm of his hand.

"I remember Doug and I watching the interview," Jennifer said. "He didn't miss a beat and the media people were fascinated. We had no idea he would be that eloquent in a crowd."

When a reporter asked Jarrett's parents if they had anything to add, they were at a loss for words. Jarrett had just about covered it all.

One of Jarrett's friends from the hospital was ushered into the room for the ceremonial first toy pick from the cart. Little Jordan was a quiet child, not at all outgoing like Jarrett. But Jarrett insisted that his buddy do the honors.

The patient looked over the hospital cart at the end of the

conference table and pondered for a minute.

"Take anything you'd like," Jarrett prodded.

That's not an easy decision for a child. The cart was overflowing with books, puzzles, action figures, games, cars and trucks, spongy balls and stuffed lions, tigers and bears.

Jordan chose a beanie baby, formed in the shape of "Lucky," the horse mascot of the local hockey team, the Kentucky Thoroughblades.

Cameras began to flash and TV crews moved in close to capture his expression. Jordan stood there mesmerized. Jarrett walked in beside him, with a smile brighter than any light provided by the media.

Next, Jarrett got behind the cart and said it was time to make the rounds. The cameras were welcome to follow.

With a hop and a limp, off he went, steering the cart down the hallway from room to room. It was like that shopping cart you always seem to get at the grocery store. One wheel seemed to have a mind of its own. Jarrett joked about his driving skills and the reporters laughed almost every step of the way.

In each room, Jarrett stopped to make his pitch to the child who was making the hospital home for now.

"You can have anything you want," he said. "It's free. Take your time. Get something good."

He sounded like a carnival barker hocking his wares:

"Step right up... have I got a deal for you..."

When a little girl automatically reached for a beanie baby, Jarrett made sure that's what she really wanted, pointing out some other "neat things" on the bottom shelf of the cart. And when a boy said he'd like to have a book, Jarrett reached under a stack and pulled out 'Treasure Island.'

"I'd recommend this one," he said. "Robert Louis Stevenson is a really good writer."

Again, the members of the media laughed. Not only was Jarrett a pint-sized Santa Claus, he was a literary critic too.

After each room had been visited and the journalists were long gone, Jennifer took Jarrett to lunch at KFC.

"We were in high spirits, laughing about the turnout and all that had happened," Jennifer said. "All of a sudden, a firefighter came over to our table and said he wanted to shake Jarrett's hand.

"He said, 'You're Jarrett Mynear, aren't you?'"

The pair couldn't believe the instant recognition. The firefighter had just heard a story about The Joy Cart on the radio and Jarrett's distinctive voice and artificial leg gave away his identity in the restaurant.

The fireman told Jarrett to keep up the good work.

Celebrity was something the Mynears would have to get used to. Soon, Jarrett couldn't go anywhere in central Kentucky without being recognized.

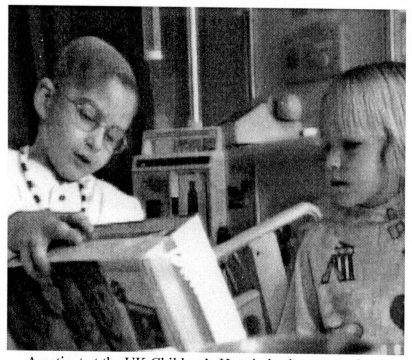

A patient at the UK Children's Hospital selects a toy from Jarrett's Joy Cart

25
My Turn

The videotape from that news conference is what struck me as undercoverage. Even though the event was well attended and received numerous mentions in the local media, I couldn't help but believe Jarrett's Joy Cart deserved more in-depth coverage.

I arranged to go to the hospital two months later–after the cart had made a few runs–for a progress report. Although Jarrett was charming in the first stories, it was a staged setting. I wanted to talk to him one-on-one, without four other cameras and stacks of microphones stuck in his face.

My videographer, Jeff Knight, and I pulled into the loading zone in front of the University of Kentucky Hospital just as the Mynears were unloading their van.

We quickly made our introductions. Jarrett said he already knew who I was. He was often allowed to stay up long enough to watch at least part of the Fox 56 Ten O'clock News, the show I anchor each weeknight.

He called me to the back of the van and excitedly began to show me all the new things he had to add to his cart that week. His sister Claire also ran right up to me like she'd known me forever. I could tell she was excited about the project too. She had been riding in the back of a van that looked like Santa's sleigh.

Eight weeks after its inaugural run, the cart wasn't running low of supplies. Quite the contrary. New donations were coming in every day. In fact, Jarrett's mother told me she would be ashamed to show me the family room at their house right then.

"There's no room to walk," she said. "We're going to have to find some storage space."

The hospital's child life specialist, Mary Kane, showed up to greet the family at the curb with three color-coded carts. The family would try to sort the toys into age-appropriate categories as they loaded the carts. One held toys for the patients under three. Another one was for those between four and ten. Then there was a cart for the older kids.

105

I told Jarrett we'd like to just follow him and watch him do his thing.

"For now, try to pretend we're not here," I told him, knowing that was not a realistic request.

Jarrett started to push the blue cart down the sidewalk, heading for the entrance to the children's wing. The cart had a loud, squeaky wheel. I remembered thinking this must seem like the ice cream truck to the kids inside. They can hear it coming and know it's full of treats.

"Oopsy," Jarrett said. I heard a bang and noticed he had struck the concrete wall as he was steering around the videographer.

"You might want to stay back a little bit," he told Jeff. "I've been known to run over people."

Upstairs, the public relations folks had already scouted out the rooms in which it was OK for us to record. Of course, when you're dealing with minors, parents have to sign permission slips, agreeing to allow their child to appear on television.

In the first room sat a little boy named Cameron. The lights were off, making the room seem dreary. He was connected to some type of monitor.

Jeff and I went in first so we could witness Jarrett's entrance. I tried to make small talk with Cameron, but he didn't speak. He just looked at us with suspicion. But when Jarrett came in and said he was giving away toys, Cameron sat up and fixed his eyes on the cart.

Jarrett steered it as close to Cameron's bed as he could and began to hold up items.

"Just let me know when you see something you like."

The boy pointed to a plastic dinosaur and Jarrett handed it to him. Cameron's grandmother, who was sitting in a chair by the door, thanked Jarrett.

"That's so nice of you," she said.

"Oh, you're welcome," said Jarrett, as he wheeled the noisy cart back out the door. "See you next time."

There came that lump in my throat again. Outwardly, two boys couldn't have been more opposite. Jarrett was outgoing and energetic; Cameron was quiet and shy. But I knew they shared a silent bond–a knowledge of what it means to be cooped up in a hospital, feeling pain and facing uncertainty.

It was a three-minute visit. But as we left that room, I looked back and noticed Cameron had propped the dinosaur next to another one he had no doubt received on Jarrett's last visit. I wondered how big his collection would grow–how many weeks he'd be there for visits from The Joy Cart.

In other rooms, Jarrett met other kids who knew him by name. Undoubtedly, every other Tuesday was a day they all had marked on their calendars. Jennifer had already told me privately they'd soon start running the cart on a weekly basis. There were enough donations to make that possible. Wouldn't that be exciting news for the long-term patients?

"How are you feeling this week, Christopher?" Jarrett said cheerfully to a five-year-old boy.

"Better," said Christopher.

"I brought you a truck like you wanted," Jarrett said.

Christopher gave Jarrett a big smile and slapped his hand with a high five.

We went into another room where a boy just couldn't seem to make up his mind. He looked over every toy three or four times. Jarrett tried his best to help with the decision, pulling out games and books from the bottom shelf and demonstrating how certain magical contraptions worked.

"How about this denim dog?" Jarrett asked. "It comes with a marker and you can get people to sign it."

"I just can't make up my mind," the boy said.

"Do you like sports?" Jarrett tried again. "Here's a sticker book about baseball."

Frankly, I was beginning to lose patience with the patient. We had a news story to shoot and Jeff had all the video we could possibly use in that room. But Jarrett never got in a hurry.

At last, the boy settled on a large poster of a monster that came with colored markers. That ought to keep him busy for a while, I thought. But I think he was through scribbling on it before we got to the next room.

"It's overwhelming for some kids," Jarrett told us. "They're afraid they'll only get one chance to pick a toy and they don't want to blow it. But the truth is, I'll see most of them again."

After we had gone to five rooms–all of the ones we had

107

permission to visit–I asked Jarrett's father to grant me an interview in a conference room. He agreed to do that while Jennifer and Jarrett continued distributing toys to the other 45 rooms on the floor.

Doug told me the story of how Jarrett was diagnosed and all he'd been through. He related the words of the child psychologist at the Mayo Clinic, the one who told them Jarrett would be the strong one through all this.

"It's true," he said. "He has indeed been the one to get us through."

Then it was Jarrett's turn. He came into the room and allowed Jeff to run a wireless microphone up his shirt. I knew immediately I could ask this nine-year-old the same kind of questions I would ask an adult. Interviewing children can be one of the most challenging things a reporter ever has to do. But talking to Jarrett was easy. Knowing where to start was the difficult part.

He told me all about "The Pink Ladies," the business plan he devised to get donations and the response he had received since the first news reports aired two months earlier.

"What's the main reason you're doing this?" I asked.

"Well," Jarrett said. "It's not really about the toys. It's about giving the kids something to look forward to.

"We went into a room the last time I was here and my dad told me the girl hadn't been out of bed for four days," Jarrett said.

"But she got out of bed and walked across the room to pick out a toy. That made me feel so great to know that I was able to do something that good."

My eyes got watery again. I noticed the public relations assistant sitting in the back of the room was also choking back tears.

I asked Jarrett if he had any advice for other children who found themselves spending a lot of time in the hospital.

"Well," he said in that high-pitched voice, "I'd tell them that they'll have some bad days, but not everything that happens in here is bad. They'll meet some good doctors and they should ask them lots of questions. They're here to help you feel better."

I asked Jarrett how long he planned to continue the project.

"As long as I'm able, both financial-wise and mental-wise, I plan to keep The Joy Cart rolling," he answered cheerfully. "And if I ever can't do it, I hope someone will keep it going in my name. I want it to be my legacy."

How many nine-year-olds know the meaning of the word *legacy?* Jarrett had a keen understanding that he had already defeated the odds. He seemed at peace with the notion that a long life is not a guarantee for any of us. *Carpe diem.*

The story wrote itself. I didn't have to do much narration. Jarrett's words and actions said more than I could ever say in a script. Jeff's video was excellent.

After I introduced the piece from the news desk a few nights later, I again watched the reaction in the studio. The man behind the teleprompter took out a handkerchief, removed his glasses and wiped his eyes.

This boy was touching people's hearts. That was a gift greater than anything he could stock on his cart.

Months later, that story won a regional Emmy. My name is on the trophy but Jarrett made the magic. As I accepted the award, I told the audience it was one of the greatest pleasures of my career to share Jarrett's story. I meant it then and I mean it now.

26
A National Audience

A member of our production department at the television station told me he'd like to send a copy of my story to one of his former girlfriends. Making videotape dubs is one of the time-consuming tasks we're always being asked to do in my business.

"Sure, I'd be glad to make you a copy," I told Dave Blair. "I'll try to get it to you in a week or two." I think I made some joke about being used to help him get back together with an old flame.

But he urged me to do it as soon as possible. He told me his ex was on the staff of The Rosie O'Donnell Show.

"This is just the kind of guest she likes to book," Dave said. "I think they'd want to have him on the show."

Dave was one of those behind-the-scenes people whom I'd seen get choked up viewing my story. I respected him a lot. But I wasn't sure about sending Jarrett's story off to a national production company. Maybe his parents wouldn't want to be bothered with it.

But the more I thought about it, the more I realized Dave was right. This was an inspiring story that could reach a national audience. I knew Jarrett could talk to anybody. He wouldn't be intimidated by the experience if the show's producers did indeed want to have him as a guest. I decided to let Dave send the tape and see if anything would become of it.

In less than a week, a New York producer was on the line to our newsroom. A woman who worked for The Rosie O'Donnell Show told us she had booked Jarrett to be on the show in just two days and she wanted all the raw tape we could provide. Our station doesn't air Rosie's show in the Lexington market and giving out raw tape was against company policy, especially if it was going to go to a program aired by one of our competitors. But the news director, who was a member of The Dream Factory board, was willing to make an exception in this case.

He knew the exposure could bring in donations and he believed Jarrett's Joy Cart definitely deserved to keep going.

Doug and Jennifer were reluctant to accept the invitation at first.

The producers called on Monday and wanted Jarrett to fly to New York on Tuesday, which would be his third day at another session of Indian Summer Camp. Jarrett loved camp and looked forward to it all year.

"If it were up to me, I would've said we'd be right there," Jennifer said. "But I wasn't sure how Jarrett would feel about it. Rosie's assistant promised they'd fly Jarrett back to Kentucky as soon as the show was over, meaning he'd only have to miss one night in his cabin."

The show was about to go on hiatus for the summer and the Mynears were told it just wasn't possible to hold the taping for another week.

Jennifer called the camp and got one of the nurses on the line.

"Jarrett was off playing somewhere, so I didn't get to tell him directly about the invitation," she said. "The nurse got all excited and began screaming to other people there in the room that Jarrett was going to be on 'The Rosie Show.'

"I said 'Wait a minute. See if Jarrett wants to do it. I won't tell them to make the reservations unless he says he's OK with leaving camp.'"

The nurse found Jarrett, relayed the message and called Jennifer back in a matter of minutes.

"His exact words were 'I'm going to New York!'" the nurse said.

The word spread quickly around camp and the other children were maybe even more excited than Jarrett.

Jarrett hadn't seen The Rosie O'Donnell Show but he knew who she was. He'd seen her on the Kids Choice Awards on Nickelodeon.

So, the whirlwind trip was on. Doug and Jennifer packed an overnight bag for each of them, and one for Jarrett. They made arrangements for a babysitter to keep Claire. They picked him up at camp, which had moved that year to Shelby County, about halfway between Lexington and Louisville. All the other kids there came out to give him a sendoff.

"Make sure you mention us on TV," more than one friend told him.

The Mynears made the 45-minute drive to the Louisville airport and flew to New York for a date with the "big time."

Like all first-time visitors to New York, Jarrett was amazed. The buildings just seemed to go on forever as he watched from the airplane window.

"There's a lot of people down there," he thought. "And a lot of them are going to see me on TV."

A stretch limousine met them at the airport and took them straight to a large hotel near the NBC Studios, where the show would be broadcast at ten o'clock the next morning. It would be shown live in New York and on taped delay to the rest of the nation.

Once they got settled, the family set out to get dinner. But they had one stop to make first. Jarrett had heard about FAO Schwarz, one of the world's premiere toy stores. A lot of people know it from the movie "Big." It's where Tom Hanks played "Heart and Soul" with his feet by jumping on a giant electronic keyboard.

The taxi pulled up and Jarrett gazed up at the building as if it were the gates of Heaven. But there was a sign on the door: *Closed For A Private Party.*

Jarrett's heart sank. He was an avid fan of "Star Wars" and "Episode One: The Phantom Menace" had just been released. He had read about a "Star Wars" display at the toy store, complete with movie props and costumes. And, as a kid who loved Lego blocks, he was determined to locate a "Star Wars" play set he hadn't been able to find in Kentucky. He was sure there was one inside that huge store, but now he'd never know.

Rosie's staff had arranged reservations at Mars 2112, a kid-friendly theme restaurant. Visitors get to the dining area by riding a flight simulator that conjures up images of outer space. The idea is to feel you've been transported to a futuristic Red Planet. Robots dance about the room and the menu lists such things as the Crater Burger and Cosmic Cheesecake.

"It was neat place," Jennifer said. "We were all fascinated by it."

But despite the fun atmosphere, Jarrett was a little quieter than usual. His family wasn't sure if it was because of the disappointment about the closed store or because he was thinking about the next day's broadcast. They knew they had butterflies and they weren't the ones who would be on stage.

When the Mynears got to the studio the next morning, staffers from Rosie's show met them at the front door. Everyone knew right away who they were and made the family feel right at home. If people in New York were supposed to be rude and uncaring, you sure couldn't have proved it at the NBC Studios that morning. They were ushered to a dressing room backstage. The star on the door displayed the name of Cheri O'Teri, a member of the Saturday Night Live ensemble.

"Wow," thought Jennifer. "This really is where the celebrities hang out."

A large fruit basket sat on a table in the room along with a tray of croissants. The refrigerator was stocked with juice, soft drinks and bottled water. It was "the royal treatment."

Production assistants subtly moved in and out of the room, quizzing Jarrett for tidbits of information. It was like a reverse police interrogation. Anything he said could and would be used in his favor.

"They were good at what they do," said Jarrett's mother. "They would slip messages to each other and leave, I guess to make notes for the show and phone calls."

The assistants found out about Jarrett's fascination with "Star Wars" and about the missed opportunity to visit FAO Schwarz. The Mynears would learn later that the conversation was more than small talk.

Jarrett was told how he was to enter the stage, where he'd sit and how he should address the cameras. One woman powdered his face. He wasn't sure about that.

He also learned he'd be in good company that day. The other guests on the roster were CBS news anchor Dan Rather, singer/actress Jennifer Lopez and Michele Williams of the television drama "Dawson's Creek." June Lockhart would also be appearing with the latest incarnation of Lassie.

Each star was in a separate dressing room, but Jarrett had an opportunity to pop his head into each room and meet the guests, basically just long enough to say hello.

"The longest visit I had was with Lassie," Jarrett laughed. "The dog plopped its head down in my lap and I couldn't get up for a few minutes. I guess you could say we bonded."

He did not meet Rosie beforehand. He was told she likes the audience to see natural first meetings.

A few minutes before ten, mom and dad wished their son good

luck and offered a last piece of advice.

"Just be yourself. It'll be over before you know it," they told him. But deep down, they were a little worried about what may come out of his mouth. Almost everything he had done on television to this point had been edited.

An assistant escorted them to a couple of seats in the audience, where they held their breath and watched the clock, getting more nervous by the minute. Backstage, Jarrett petted Lassie.

Twenty-five minutes into the show, Rosie introduced Jarrett.

"My next guest is truly inspirational. He turns rainy days into sunny ones for every child he meets. He has a heart of gold and on top of that, he's only ten years old. Please welcome Jarrett Mynear!"

The band struck up the theme music and the camera panned to the left of the stage. Jarrett, dressed in a plaid, short-sleeved shirt, limped down two steps and waved to the crowd, which applauded loudly. He carried something in his left hand, but it wasn't clear what it was. He walked to center stage where Rosie stood to meet him and shook her hand.

Jennifer and Doug sat on the edge of their seats, beaming on the outside, tied in knots on the inside.

Rosie told Jarrett she had seen the news story about him and was impressed.

"Tell everyone what you do."

"Well," began Jarrett, "I have a business that I started. I take around three carts of toys to the kids at the Children's Hospital in Kentucky."

He looked straight into the camera as he continued, like an old pro who wants to make sure the audience is included in the conversation.

"Each kid gets to pick a toy of their choice. They're brand new and so far, we've had a great response and everybody thinks it's a good idea."

If he was nervous, it didn't show.

Rosie asked Jarrett how he got the idea for the cart. He told her about his time in the Seattle hospital and how the ladies auxiliary there brought toys around.

"It always helped me look forward to something and I wasn't

quite as scared when I knew that they were coming around," he said. "I thought maybe I could do something like that to help the kids who are really scared and some of the kids who are new at this and some of the ones who are old at this."

Rosie asked him why he had been in the hospital so often. Jarrett calmly and clearly explained his three bouts with Ewing's sarcoma, once in the leg and twice in the lining of his skull.

"Then, I had myelodysplasia, which is a bone marrow cancer and it can turn into leukemia, but they got it before it did."

The audience erupted into applause with that last piece of good news. Jarrett responded with a giant smile.

Then, Rosie had her director roll some of our videotape so the audience could see Jarrett in action, taking toys from room to room at the UK Children's Hospital.

"Were the kids surprised when you first showed up with the toys?" the host asked.

"Yes," answered Jarrett. "One of the fathers of one of the kids tried to pull out his wallet and was wondering how much the toy cost. I said it was free. You don't have to pay for anything on the cart."

"Well, Jarrett, that brings up a good point. How do you get all these brand new toys?"

"I have some private donors who give money and donate some toys, too," he said. "I've contacted businesses and stores that have been really nice to donate toys."

"Where do you keep all the toys?"

"In our family room."

"In your family room?" Rosie asked, wide-eyed and incredulously.

"That's right," Jarrett laughed. Then he turned and looked straight into the camera again. His voice raised an octave and several decibels as he spread out his hands for emphasis.

"And if anybody can, WE NEED SOMEONE TO DONATE A WAREHOUSE!"

The audience broke out in loud laughter.

"Guess what, Jarrett?" Rosie said. "You now have a warehouse and Toys R Us is going to stock it with as many toys as you need."

Jarrett's eyes got big and his smile even bigger. He seemed

speechless, but the audience could read his lips as he mouthed "Oh my gosh."

"You keep doing what you do," Rosie ordered. "I think it's a great thing."

Then she prompted him to talk about the little girl who hadn't gotten out of bed for days–the same story he had told me during our interview.

"She got up and got something off the cart and ran back to bed and started playing with it. I just thought that was so nice. I'm glad I can make that much of a difference in these kids' lives."

He said it humbly, not boastfully.

"We're glad you can too, Jarrett," said Rosie. "Very glad."

Then she touched on another subject dear to Jarrett's heart. She held up a picture of his cabin mates from Indian Summer Camp, relating how they had whisked Jarrett away from one of his favorite places on a day's notice.

"That must be a special camp you go to," she said.

"Yes, it's a camp for cancer kids. And this is my cabin. Cabin Number Eleven!" Jarrett announced with enthusiasm.

Everyone applauded for Cabin Number Eleven. Jarrett knew his buddies would be watching with pride back in Kentucky.

Then Rosie mentioned that she'd heard Jarrett had wanted to go to FAO Schwarz.

"Yes," he said. "I was going to get all this "Star Wars" stuff and they were closed for a special meeting."

"They were closed!" Rosie seemed indignant. "Were you going to get it for you or the kids at the hospital or both?"

"Both," Jarrett laughed sheepishly. "I'm looking for this Lego set and I can't find it in Kentucky."

Rosie instructed Jarrett to say "abracadabra."

"Abracadabra," Jarrett obeyed, watching as Rosie reached beneath her desk. She pulled out a "Star Wars" Lego set and handed it to the boy.

"Whoaaa!" Jarrett exclaimed, again turning temporarily speechless.

In the audience, Doug and Jennifer marveled at how the staffers had picked up on everything they'd heard in the dressing room and made magic happen in such a short span of time.

"I guess you have to watch what you say around here," Jennifer whispered to her husband.

Back on stage, it was obvious Rosie was about to wrap up the interview. It had gone six minutes, which is about standard for a segment on a television talk show.

"I have a gift for you, too," Jarrett told Rosie.

"What do you have for me?"

He reached beside his seat and held up that item he had carried out from backstage.

"At Indian Summer Camp this year, there was a special gift for each kid. This is a flashlight and when you pull on it, it turns into a lantern," he said as he demonstrated. "I signed it for you."

Again, the audience roared its approval.

"I thank you very much, mister. Give me a high five."

Jarrett slapped Rosie's hand.

"I'll treasure it always," she said. "It was nice to meet you, honey. Keep up the good work."

"Great meeting you," Jarrett said.

And the show went to a commercial break.

Doug and Jennifer got up from their seats to go meet their son backstage. They knew he had just been given a dose of medicine that was better than anything in a bottle.

It was like a booster shot of spirit.

After the show, Rosie came back out on stage to pose for pictures with the guests and audience members and to sign autographs.

Doug and Jennifer met her.

"She was wonderful," Jennifer said. "She talked to us like we'd known her for years. In fact, everyone from the show came back out and just made over Jarrett, telling him what a good job he did. It was obvious they were smitten with him."

Rosie pulled Jennifer aside.

"I want to know how he's *really* doing," Rosie said.

Jennifer told her Jarrett's situation was always a "one day at a time" thing.

"But right now, things really are looking up."

"I'll keep in touch," Rosie said. And in the months to come, she was true to that promise.

117

The family made another friend that day, someone who, like Rosie, continued to call and check on Jarrett's progress long after the taping was a distant memory. Joey Kola was the audience coach, the one who comes out before the show and tells jokes, encourages applause and goes over the "rules" of being in a studio audience.

He came up to Jarrett afterward, with tears in his eyes.

"I'm as sincere as I've ever been," he told the ten-year-old. "I've met a lot of stars on this show, and big name athletes, but it means more to me to meet you than all of them put together. People say those people are heroes. To me, you're what's really a hero."

Jarrett and Rosie O'Donnell, June 1999

27
Toyland

As the Mynears gathered their things to leave the NBC studios, a production assistant came up to them and asked how much time they had before they had to head to the airport.

Doug checked his watch and said they had about 90 minutes to kill.

"Good," the assistant said. "How would you like to go to FAO Schwarz?"

As had happened so often that morning, a big smile crossed Jarrett's face. Someone at the world's largest toy store had just seen the live broadcast of The Rosie O'Donnell Show and called to offer the Mynears a private tour. The CEO wanted Jarrett to be his guest. He had been impressed by the young man and dismayed that he had been unable to visit the night before.

Even Rosie's staff, which was used to pulling off all kinds of surprises, was caught off guard by the call.

A limo was already waiting out front.

So off they went. In a matter of minutes, the car pulled up in front of the store and a man dressed like a giant toy soldier opened the limo door and escorted the family to the store's entrance.

"There were a lot of tourists standing around on the plaza," Jennifer laughed. "No doubt, they were wondering what celebrity had just arrived. Maybe they thought it was going to be Michael Jackson or Macaulay Culkin. Then we got out. They had to wonder who in the world we were."

Surprisingly, a couple of people knew.

Doug overheard one woman say, "I just saw that boy on the Rosie show." And another woman approached the Mynears to let them know she was from Louisville. She had seen stories about Jarrett back home in Kentucky.

That's the power of television. Instant recognition. It was an Andy Warhol moment.

"I thought to myself what a whirlwind we were in," Jennifer said. "On Monday, I had been washing floors at home. I got a phone call from New York and now it was 48 hours later and we were in the spotlight. It was surreal."

Inside, the store's CEO, several managers and the marketing director greeted the family and told Jarrett how honored they were that he wanted to visit their store. Then they whisked him straight to the "Star Wars" room. The first thing Jarrett noticed was the Darth Maul costume.

His mom described his reaction as "bug-eyed."

Every piece of "Star Wars" merchandise ever produced must've been in that room.

As Jarrett studied the displays, both the manager and an assistant manager came up with baskets in their hands.

"Let's pick some things out," they told Jarrett. "Get anything you want."

"Thanks so much," Jarrett said. "Some of this stuff will be so cool to have on The Joy Cart."

"No, we mean pick some things out for yourself," the manager said. "We're going to take care of The Joy Cart too, but right now we want to treat you."

As they walked the aisles, the managers kept pointing to things, asking Jarrett if he'd like to have this or that.

"It's funny," his mother said. "They almost had to make him take things. He was just overwhelmed. He really must've thought he didn't deserve all the attention. I would've guessed that he'd have taken everything he could get his hands on. But he wasn't greedy at all. The people in the store really wanted to pile on the gifts."

As they walked through the various rooms, one of the employees learned that Jarrett had a sister back home. So, they took him to the Madeline room so he could pick out a doll for Claire.

Then Jarrett noticed a large stuffed frog.

"My granny would love that."

The manager asked why he thought so.

Jarrett told them that Granny Jeanne had given him several small frogs over the years. She told him to sit them on the dressers in his hospital rooms. When he looked at the frogs, she wanted him to think of her and know that she was always thinking of him.

"Well, let's wrap it up for her," the manager said.

"Jarrett," his mother interrupted. "We'll never be able to get that big thing back on the plane."

She was told not to worry about that. The store would ship everything out that afternoon. It would arrive in Kentucky by courier the next day.

Time was running out, but the folks in the store had one more place to show Jarrett. It was a private room that was more like a museum of the world's most exclusive and expensive toys. It was a place for celebrities, not open to the public.

The room contained a toy Mercedes Benz and $25,000 dolls bedecked with jewels. Each corner contained virtual reality games and some of the most elaborate pinball machines ever built. A massive model train display took up a large portion of floor space. Everything was turned on and Jarrett was allowed to play with anything he wanted.

It was the stuff fairy tales are made of– *"The Frog and the Little Prince: Chapter One– The Secret Chamber."*

Jarrett had been in a hurry to get back to camp, but that was before he discovered the hidden rooms of FAO Schwarz. He could've stayed there well into the night.

On the way out of the store, the Mynears passed through the candy department. One of the assistants asked Jennifer how many kids were at Jarrett's camp.

When she found out it was about 80, she didn't blink an eye.

"Let's send something back for them," the assistant said.

She suggested a new type of lollipop that used batteries in the handle. When you placed the candy in your mouth, you could hear a radio play in your head.

Jarrett sampled one and thought it was pretty cool. So, they bagged up 80 of them and handed them to Jarrett. Once again, he was going to get to play Santa Claus.

By early evening, the Mynears pulled into Indian Summer Camp. Jarrett–in fact, everyone–was exhausted. But it was a hero's welcome.

One of the meeting rooms had been turned into a party room. All of the campers came in for ice cream and they watched a tape of Jarrett's appearance with Rosie. Jarrett grinned from ear to ear as he saw his interview played back for the first time. Everyone cheered when he mentioned the camp.

Then he passed out the suckers and 80 kids spent the next hour listening to voices in their heads.

Night fell and everyone made their way back to their cabins, using their special camp flashlights.

As he approached Cabin Number Eleven, Jarrett wondered if Rosie was using the one he'd given her.

28
Response

The talk show appearance opened the floodgates of goodwill. Jarrett's family began to receive donations and letters from across the country.

"Vacation Bible Schools from all over Kentucky told us they wanted to make The Joy Cart their fundraising project," Jennifer said. "We'd get checks for $1,000 or $1,500. The teachers would attach letters saying they'd never collected that much before."

The toy cart was something to which kids everywhere could relate. They could really see how their money was being put to good use and a lot of them emptied their piggy banks to help.

Jarrett's Joy Cart also became the pet project for countless civic groups. Just as Rosie had announced, a warehouse became available in Lexington, donated by Rob McGoodwin of McGoodwin Records Management. The company's employees hauled several pickup truck loads of toys out of the Mynears' basement and family room to the new wide-open space. And within a couple of weeks, a tractor trailer pulled up to the warehouse, loaded with games, puzzles, dolls and stuffed animals from Toys R Us.

"Looking at it, it was hard to imagine that I had worried so that we wouldn't be able to keep the toy cart going after a couple of trips," Jennifer said. "It was overwhelming."

Now, not only did they have enough toys to give out 50 each week at the UK Children's Hospital, they had extras to give to charity auctions, to families that had been burned out of their homes, to a shelter for abused children and runaways, and to Christmas toy drives. They also put smaller items in the Kentucky Clinic's "treasure chest." Now, when kids came in for chemotherapy, CT scans or any type of specialty need, they could take home toy cars, beanie babies or plastic action figures as a reward for good behavior.

Each year, the American Cancer Society sponsors hundreds of fundraisers around the country. Relay for Life is the biggest one in communities from coast to coast. Participants solicit donations and walk for miles, often around a high school track.

At the 1999 relay in Lexington, Jarrett was the star. His friend, Kathy Tabb, had asked him to read the mission statement before the walkers took off around the track at Henry Clay High School.

Jarrett stood at the microphone and read how the ACS works to "offer hope, progress and answers" to those who battle the world's most widespread disease.

"Here was this little person standing there not ashamed that he didn't have hair, not self-conscious of his size or hung up in any way about his condition," Kathy said. "Just the few words he had to say made more of an impact than anything anyone else could've done. I had more than a few adults say Jarrett has changed the entire way they look at having cancer."

After his opening remarks, Jarrett grabbed a corner of a banner that said "Cancer Survivors Thank You for Your Support" and led the walkers around the track. He wore sunglasses, a cap that was turned backward and shorts–not embarrassed at all that his prosthesis was showing. Except for the artificial leg, he looked just like any other cool kid hanging out behind the school.

"After that, I couldn't believe how many people sought him out just to shake his hand or get his autograph," Kathy said. "They were gushing over him as if he was the biggest movie star or athlete in the world. He was giving pep talks left and right."

She realized then that her young friend's giving wasn't just in the form of toys. The way he inspired people was greater than any gift one could hold in their hands.

That fall, Jarrett's classmates at West Jessamine Middle School sponsored their first major toy drive. They set up a Giving Tree in the school's lobby and kids were encouraged to take a tag from its branches. The tags were generic enough, saying things as simple as "Buy a gift appropriate for a five-year-old girl" or "Buy a book that would interest a ten-year-old boy."

Most kids went above and beyond what the tags said. If they were asked to buy a book, many of them bought ten books instead.

"That's what was so dumbfounding to us," Jennifer said. "We didn't know how it would mushroom and affect everyone in the school. The generosity was infectious. Jarrett may've looked different than the other kids and he was about half their size, but they saw how he was reaching out and wanted to be a part of it."

Many of the school's clubs, such as the Future Community Career Leaders of America, got involved in the drive. Long after the last tag was taken off the tree, students were still collecting toys.

"I've never seen anything bring a school together like that," said Jennifer, who had been a teacher for years. "When I'd walk into the school with Jarrett, it never ceased to amaze me the reaction he'd get. Everyone stopped to talk to him."

Every school has its cliques–close-knit groups of students who are considered to be bookworms and nerds, and those who are jocks and the "popular people." Jarrett seemed to fit into any group. He was never shunned and seldom teased among his peers.

Students yelled their greetings from the other end of hallways, gave him high fives and offered to open doors or carry his books any time they could.

"I came close to crying so many times just by walking down the hall," Jarrett's mother said. "Everyone made sure Jarrett fit in. In fact, he had become a leader. The principal once introduced him at an assembly as someone who was small in stature but huge in heart. Those words really made Jarrett feel good."

Jarrett and his mother were asked to visit the students in the Alternative School, a separate area for those who had difficulty adjusting to the structure of a classroom. Many of the kids were from broken homes and had already been in trouble with the law. They were prone to fights, destined to drop out and generally didn't care that much about homework or class rank.

"But when we went in there, the kids couldn't have been sweeter," Jennifer said. "They showed us great respect. They called me 'Mrs. Mynear' and offered me their chairs. They all shook Jarrett's hand and many of them said they'd be bringing toys in to help. Their teachers were amazed. They said they'd never seen the kids pay so much attention to a guest."

There really was something magical about Jarrett. He tore down walls, made mean people nice, tough people cry, and sad people smile.

When the toy drive ended, the gifts were stacked taller than the tree and pretty much took over the lobby. It was the definition of school pride, embodied in boxes and bags.

As the collection effort wound down, Jarrett's family received another stack of papers to fill out. But these documents didn't outline the risks of experimental surgeries, have anything to do with insurance or drug plans, or contain medical terms and procedures with definitions too complicated to comprehend.

It was a nomination form for a major national award. Kathy Tabb, who later became president of the local chapter of the American Cancer Society, presented it to the Mynears. It was a big surprise. Kathy had secretly worked to push Jarrett's name for the Prudential Spirit of Community Awards.

One hundred four students would be chosen nationwide to compete for ten national medals. The finalists would include two students from each state, the District of Columbia and Puerto Rico. Half of them would be middle-schoolers and the other half would come from the high school level.

The Prudential Insurance Company received more than 20,000 applications.

"We were glad to fill out the forms– mostly as a favor to Kathy– but we didn't really think too much about winning," Jennifer said. "The odds against it were incredible and there were so many worthy applicants."

But the word came in February that Jarrett would be Kentucky's middle school winner. Prudential wanted to make the presentation in front of the student body at Jarrett's school.

The principal called an assembly, but the students didn't really know what was up.

A representative of the insurance company took the microphone and began to talk about the award and what community spirit meant. The kids caught on pretty quickly. They began to whisper that "it must be for Jarrett." They spied Jarrett's parents in the back of the room.

And in less than ten minutes, their suspicions were confirmed. When Jarrett was called to the podium, a cheer went up that could've raised the roof off the school. The students and teachers jumped to their feet and applauded loudly as the visitor placed a large silver medallion over Jarrett's head.

It was seen as an award for the whole school and, in part, it was.

The response to the toy drive had been one of the factors that made an impression on the judges.

"I have something else for Jarrett," the presenter continued. "Here's a check for $1,000."

More applause and open-mouthed expressions resulted. That was an awfully big number to put on a check. To the students, it might as well have been a million dollars.

"And Jarrett gets an all-expenses paid trip to Washington, D.C. This May, he'll represent Jessamine County and Kentucky in the national competition."

Jarrett was on cloud nine as his classmates patted him on the back and asked to see the medal.

He wasn't sure he could win at a higher level. His classmates didn't see how he could lose.

29
Common Bond

Jarrett's circle of friends included a lot of kids with cancer. When he'd wheel The Joy Cart into a room at the UK Children's Hospital, Jarrett's first question to a new patient was almost always, "What are you in here for?"

He would compare notes with the children, asking them which doctors they knew, how long they'd be taking chemotherapy and so on.

"Well, hang in there. It's not so bad," he'd say. "I've been through it four times."

You could see apprehension vanish as Jarrett talked to the patients, completely tuning out the other adults in the room. Many scared kids realized that if this little guy could handle it, so could they.

Jarrett actually began those goodwill visits around the hospital months before he began thinking about The Joy Cart.

In 1997, Jarrett met Charles Ballard Wolford, a boy who was five years older than him, from the small eastern Kentucky town of Phelps. Everyone called him C.B.

C.B. also had Ewing's sarcoma. A few weeks after he began his chemotherapy, his weight dropped from 90 pounds to 59 pounds. He had violent reactions to the treatment, throwing up several times a day. According to his mother, Faye Wolford, C.B. completely lost his will to live.

"He was really depressed," Faye said. "He wouldn't talk. He wouldn't do anything. He said he wanted to die."

Enter Jarrett.

The pint-sized cheerleader learned that C.B. had given up hope. So, he made a visit to his room.

"He pops in the door and says, 'Hey man, you're not dead yet. Let's have some fun,'" Faye said. "He wanted C.B. to play Nintendo with him."

But C.B. said he didn't feel like it.

"Yeah, yeah, come on," Jarrett insisted. "I need somebody to beat."

Faye recalls an instant change in C.B's demeanor.

"C.B. was sitting there looking at this little guy who's been through everything he's been through... same cancer... and he came out of that bed and started playing video games. From that moment on, this kid did not stop."

She watched the two boys as they laughed and played for more than an hour.

"It was like a miracle. It was wonderful," she said. "Jarrett gave me my boy back."

Jarrett and C.B. had many discussions about what to anticipate with the bone marrow transplant and how he could expect to feel after taking different medicines.

The two became close pals, not only around the hospital, but also at summer camp.

As C.B.'s condition worsened, he decided to write a book. He called it simply, "My Story About Cancer." That effort gained him a lot of attention.

Through a chain of events that began with a pen pals program at the hospital, news of C.B's book made it to an aide at The White House. On a chilly October morning in 1998, C.B. picked up the phone at his home and mumbled a few words into the receiver.

He called to his mother: "Mom, it's The White House. They want to speak to you."

According to the book, Faye told him to quit kidding around.

"No really, Mom, I think it's for real," C.B. said.

Faye took the phone and listened as a liaison for President Clinton invited the family to come to Washington for a visit.

Faye began to cry. C.B. had dreamed of meeting the president, but she never believed it would be possible.

Friends and family members, as well as people from the hospital (including the Mynears), pitched in to help pay for a trip to the nation's capital. On October 11th, C.B. toured The White House and sat in on the president's weekly radio address to the nation. After the broadcast, Mr. Clinton came over and introduced himself to C.B. They posed for pictures and C.B. got to sit in the president's chair. According to his mother, the young man was extremely sick that day, but he put on a brave face, telling the president he was doing well.

Just 16 days later, C.B. died.

In the months that followed, his mother finished his book.

That spring, as a school day ended at West Jessamine Middle School, Jarrett went to the car where his mother was waiting for him.

She held a book.

"I want you to look at this," Jennifer said, handing the book to Jarrett.

It was "My Story About Cancer" by Charles B. Wolford.

"Look inside," she instructed.

Jarrett opened the cover and read the dedication:

"To my best friend, Jarrett."

==========

Response to Jarrett's first appearance on The Rosie O'Donnell Show had been so great that the producers decided to invite him back for an update in February 2000.

Jarrett said he'd love to come back and he wanted to mention C.B.'s book.

So the producers also invited Faye Wolford to be a guest.

Doug and Jennifer enjoyed escorting Faye and her sister-in-law around the Big Apple. It was the first time they had seen the skyscrapers of New York City and it was a delight for the women from the coalfields of eastern Kentucky.

"We all laughed constantly," Jennifer said. "We looked like the typical tourists, with our necks craned upward and our jaws gaping open at the sights. Doug was determined to show them as much as he could in one night. He wore us all out the night before the show."

They went to the top of the Empire State Building, to Radio City Music Hall and through Times Square. They were out until midnight.

It didn't matter. No one could sleep anyway.

During the warm-up before the live broadcast the next morning, one man in the audience seemed disappointed when he heard the topic would be "people who make a difference."

He yelled out that he wanted to see celebrities.

Jennifer said the audience coach–their friend Joey Kola– went off on the man.

"Let me tell you," Joey said emphatically, "these people you'll see today are more like stars than anyone you could ever meet!"

As the segment about Jarrett was introduced, a videotape played that gave the audience background about his relationship with C.B.

The tape included a home video clip with C.B. near the end of his life, with sunken cheeks and pale skin. He said, in a weak voice with a heavy Southern accent, "The way I feel is you fight until you can't fight no more."

Then Jarrett appeared on the tape, with tears streaming down his face, saying, "I just want everybody to know that he was a great boy and that he wanted to help everyone. I think that's great."

Jarrett and Faye received warm applause as the tape ended and the cameras cut to them live on stage.

Faye told how C.B. had mentioned to her as soon as he started the book that he wanted to dedicate it to Jarrett.

"I asked him why," Faye said softly, "and he said, 'Jarrett just inspires me.'"

Faye took Jarrett's hand and Jarrett's smile reached from ear to ear. They both felt C.B's spirit was with them.

Then Rosie called attention to the silver medallion hanging around Jarrett's neck.

"What's that new necklace you're wearing? Are you stylin'?" she teased.

"No, I don't wear ten-ton weights just for style," Jarrett said, laughing.

"Good, good," said Rosie. "So what is it? Did you win the Olympics?"

Jarrett explained that he was a local winner of the Prudential Spirit of Community award and that he would soon be going to Washington to compete for a national honor.

Again, loud applause filled the studio.

"And what does that say about volunteering?" Rosie prompted.

Jarrett ended the show with great words of wisdom.

"I think anybody, no matter what age they are, can get into volunteering–that they can help somebody. That completes your life. It makes it worthwhile."

30
Metal Head

"Routine scans" became a dreaded term for the Mynears. Doctors used the phrase to mean there's nothing to worry about; "We're just checking to make sure everything's as good as we think it is." But so many times the results had meant the *routine* would be months of chemo treatments and radiation. Each time Jarrett's parents took him in for a MRI, a CT scan or an x-ray, there was a nervousness in the air. Too many times the films showed mysterious dark spots in bones and tissue.

On March 27, 2000, just three weeks from Jarrett's eleventh birthday, the *routine* played out again.

This time the scans showed cancer had returned in the lining of Jarrett's skull and was dangerously close to the brain.

Ewing's sarcoma was back for the fourth time.

"We were scared to death," Jarrett's mother recalled. "Now the doctors were talking about making incisions in the back of Jarrett's head–cuts that would be just centimeters from his brain."

They wondered if just a little slip of the hand could result in permanent brain damage. But, again, they were overcome with that inevitable feeling of blind faith. What other choice did they have?

"The doctors were careful to stress to us that this was in the *lining* of the skull and the *lining* of the brain, not in the brain itself," Jennifer said. The indication was that it would move into the brain if they didn't act soon.

So, within a week, Jarrett was back on the operating table. The doctors made a slit down the back of his head and pulled the skin apart. They removed a piece of bone from his skull about two inches in diameter and scraped tumor tissue off the brain's lining.

The operation went on for a half day, as the surgeons worked with care and precision. Jarrett's head was in a vice to keep him from moving even the slightest bit while he slept.

When they were certain they had removed as much of the cancerous tissue as possible, the doctors sized a piece of metal to put in Jarrett's head to replace the missing section of skull. That act meant a new nickname for the boy. In the weeks and months to come, Jennifer began calling Jarrett "Titanium Cranium" whenever they got into a good-natured teasing match.

Anyone who looked closely could see the screws under the skin on Jarrett's head and, in typical fashion, he made the most of his unique circumstances. Jarrett liked to shock people by telling them about the metal plate and showing them its outline.

He told airport security guards that he was "their walking nightmare." If the plate in his head didn't set off metal detectors, his prosthesis was sure to. He was the "bionic man." If he was going to set off bells and whistles at the airport, he might as well enjoy the attention. He left guards and everyone behind him laughing each time he finally got clearance to pass through the checkpoints.

He would walk through the metal detector with his hands straight in front of him and step without bending at the knees—just like Frankenstein's monster, groaning and glaring straight ahead. He had a knack of turning awkward moments into light-hearted encounters.

For several weeks, Jarrett received low levels of radiation beamed at his head.

"We worried about that, too," Jennifer said. "We were told that skin and bone could break down over time, but the doctors ended that treatment just as soon as they felt they could."

More chemotherapy followed, this time using Taxotere injections, a drug that was considered non-invasive and one that didn't affect Jarrett's quality of life. It didn't make him nauseous or zap his energy.

The chemo was to attack a part of the tumor that couldn't be removed during the surgery and any trace cancerous cells in the body. According to Dr. Jeffrey Moscow, UK's chief of pediatric hematology/oncology, that section of the tumor was attached to a large vein that drains part of the brain. The surgeons were concerned that if they'd enter that space it would cause draining they couldn't control.

Jarrett rebounded quickly, shunning the helmet his radiologist wanted him to wear. Life's a journey and Jarrett intended to stay on the road. He had a lot of appearances and trips coming up and he wasn't about to miss them.

Jarrett was a man of steel and he could tap on his head to prove it.

31
Medal Winner

In May, the Mynears went to Washington. It was still amazing to them that Jarrett's Joy Cart project had won them trips to New York and now, the nation's capital.

Along with the Prudential honor came four days of touring museums and historic sites, and several programs and seminars on volunteerism.

As the Mynears checked into the Marriott hotel in McLean, Virginia–headquarters for the ceremonies– they were separated from their son.

"We found out right away that for the next four days, the kids would stay together and the parents would stay together, but the two groups would have little contact," Jennifer said. "Jarrett was matched up with Matthew Nonnemacher, a twelve-year-old from Pennsylvania. Our rooms wouldn't even be on the same floor."

She praised the arrangement, saying it really helped the children hone their social skills.

"It was a fantastic experience. The kids made friends instantly," she said. "I'd never seen Jarrett so emotionally-charged in his life."

On the first night, the students went through several ice-breaking exercises. They played games and then told about their own projects, the ones that had won them the honor to be there.

Jarrett cherished the interaction.

"My friends at school could talk about the toy cart, but they couldn't really relate to my reasons for doing what I do," Jarrett said. "But these kids were like me. It was so easy to talk to them about anything."

The group was described as the brains behind 104 amazing ideas.

There were kids who started food kitchens in their neighborhoods, a boy who tested the quality of residential well water in his community, those who devised anti-violence programs in their schools and provided tutoring for slow learners. One girl collected suitcases for foster children who always seemed to be on the move after reading that many of them had to tote their belongings in plastic garbage bags. And there was Ryan Tripp, the famous "Lawnmower Boy" from Utah who drew attention to the need for organ donors by mowing the lawns of capitol buildings in all 50 states.

One high school senior from Redmond, Washington instantly became Jarrett's buddy. Paul Gordon had raised thousands of dollars for transplant patients and had become a national spokesman about the importance of organ donation. A year later, he would produce a documentary about young role models which included a profile of Jarrett.

"Everybody was pumped to be there," Jarrett said.

The week included a boat cruise on the Potomac River, a breakfast at the Capitol with U.S. senators and representatives, and a wreath-laying ceremony at the Tomb of the Unknown Soldier in Arlington National Cemetery.

On the second night, Senator John Glenn spoke to the group during a reception in the rotunda of the Museum of Natural History. Jarrett loved it. It was surreal to hear from one of the nation's space pioneers as he stood in the shadow of a giant wooly mammoth. The prehistoric past combined with 20th century history as an astronaut spoke about his accomplishments to those who would be leaders in the 21st century.

After the speech, many of the students went into a side room to have their pictures taken with the senator. As he waited his turn, Jarrett made another friend on the spot. His parents were shocked to see him walk out of the room holding the hand of a high-profile woman.

"Mom, Dad," Jarrett said. "This is Annie Glenn. She wanted to meet you."

And so they met the senator's wife. Doug and Jennifer never knew with whom their son was going to strike up a conversation.

Each day as the nominees loaded onto buses to visit monuments and landmarks, the parents would do the same thing–but on different buses with different destinations.

"It was amusing to see the adults heading in one direction and the kids going the other way," Jennifer said. "We would wave and acknowledge each other and then wouldn't see each other again for hours."

It gave Jarrett a sense of freedom and responsibility.

The parents had no worries. Principals and school administrators from all over the country were there to serve as chaperones.

On the third day, all of the families gathered at the Reagan Building for the awards luncheon.

"Parents kept coming up to me and saying, 'You know Jarrett is going to be one of the winners, don't you?'" Jennifer said. "I didn't feel that way. All of the kids were winners and I didn't see that he stood above any of them."

When Jarrett walked into the banquet hall, Jennifer gasped. She hadn't even been able to go to his room that morning to help him get ready for the ceremony.

There he stood, looking nice in his black suit and tie, but his shirttail wasn't completely tucked in and he had on blue sneakers. A baseball cap topped off the ensemble.

She looked at Doug and rolled her eyes. He laughed and said, "That's our boy!"

When the emcee announced the ten winners, sure enough Jarrett's name was called.

"It was mind-boggling," Jennifer said. "When I looked around that room and thought about all the things those 104 kids had accomplished, I was so proud, not only of Jarrett but of America's youth. It was uplifting and reassuring.

"All of the kids were cheering. They celebrated each other."

In just three days, Jarrett had become close with three of the other four middle school winners. That made the celebration even more exciting.

There he stood on stage, now with a gold medallion around his neck and a baseball cap pulled down so far you couldn't see his eyes. But you could see a big smile.

The award included a $5,000 check to be used toward Jarrett's education. He also received a crystal bowl, etched with a drawing of children holding hands all around the rim.

When the ceremony ended, the other nominees were bused back to the hotel. But the winners stayed behind for pictures, radio interviews and to give quotes to be dropped into press releases. Once again, Jarrett wowed the reporters with his eloquence. In fact, his parents had trouble pulling him away. He wanted to talk to anyone and everyone who would listen.

"If I can do something like this, anyone can," he told the interviewers. "Volunteering just makes me feel so good."

You can bet that quote got used over and over by the public relations folks at Prudential.

"He was electrified," Jennifer said. "There's no doubt about it. I wouldn't take anything for that experience for him."

There was still another day of activities after the awards were handed out and it held another lesson for Jarrett.

"I thought some of the kids might be jealous or down in the dumps about not winning," he said. "But the ones who didn't win were still nice. It was kind of weird. There was no jealousy."

Jarrett saw what it was like to be gracious in defeat. But really, it was a reflection of how he'd been all his life. Each time he had been given disappointing news, he had refused to be down about it. He had always looked for things to celebrate.

32
Chance Meetings

Jarrett left Washington, knowing he'd back in just one month. He had learned earlier that year that he was a local recipient of a Jefferson Award.

The American Institute for Public Service each year recognizes people who encourage community involvement. The program has been around since 1962, when Jacqueline Kennedy Onassis, Senator Robert Taft, Jr., and philanthropist Sam Beard founded it. On the local level, media sponsors nominate ordinary people who do extraordinary things. WKYT-TV, the CBS affiliate in Lexington, nominated Jarrett. News Director Jim Ogle wrote that "Jarrett can inspire a room full of people more than any adult I've ever heard." Jarrett was one of 41 local winners from more than 14,000 nominees nationwide.

There are also national winners–celebrities and politicians who have a long history of fostering public service. Past winners include former secretary of state Dr. Henry Kissinger, tennis great Arthur Ashe and Supreme Court Justice Thurgood Marshall. The 2000 winners included country singer Faith Hill, who had established an adult literacy program, and Dr. Benjamin Carson, a world-renowned pediatric surgeon at John Hopkins University Hospital. Another familiar name appeared on the winner's list. U.S. Senator John Glenn would be recognized for his public service. Jarrett was in elite company.

This trip allowed for winners to bring just one guest, so Doug and Claire stayed behind. Most of the winners were adults who brought spouses.

From the time they checked into the Loews L'Enfant Plaza Hotel and were ushered to the opening night cocktail reception, Jarrett and his mother could tell this was a highly formal and prestigious affair. It was a completely different atmosphere than the Prudential ceremony a month earlier, where kids roamed the halls in T-shirts and shorts.

Jarrett felt a little uncomfortable at first, but at the reception each winner was asked to give a one-minute speech about their project. Again, he was impressed by all the good ideas these people had. There were people who established adult reading programs, those who opened clinics in poor inner city neighborhoods and athletes who spent countless hours in anti-drug outreach programs.

"They were adults who had the same motivations as he did," his mother said. "Before, he had mostly been exposed to kids who were working on projects through their schools or on their summer breaks."

Jarrett, who made friends quickly everywhere he went, did it again that first night at the hotel. After the reception, he struck up a conversation with another of the local award winners, Greg Forbes Siegman, a former substitute teacher from Chicago. The 27-year-old had been mentioned in more than 200 media reports and was one of the country's most celebrated volunteers.

Greg's story began in 1997 when he ran into two of his African-American students who lived in the Chicago projects and invited them into a restaurant to join him for milkshakes. The restaurant catered to mostly affluent white customers. When Greg and the students sat down, he noticed a woman at the next table look at them in disdain and move her purse out of reach. It made him furious and he vowed to turn the negative into a positive. Since then, he had never missed a week of bringing different kids together for milkshakes. His "BrunchBunch.com" program included hundreds of students and adults from different races, cultures and financial backgrounds. The lunches took place in more than 50 of Chicago's nicest restaurants, and from that effort Greg was able to form a foundation that gives scholarships to deserving need-based students. He called it the 11-10-02 Foundation, naming it for his 30th birth date. Greg wanted the name to symbolize how much can be accomplished by people in their younger years.

During a group photo session following the reception, Greg was asked to kneel down on the floor with the four youth winners while the adult winners stood behind them.

"I was embarrassed," Greg said, not really seriously. "I had gone there determined to act like an adult, even though I was the youngest of the adult winners. And here was the photographer lumping me in with the kids. But it turned out to be a blessing because that's how I met Jarrett."

"Greg and Jarrett just hit if off," Jennifer said. "Jarrett loved hearing Greg's stories and, even though he had done such important things, Greg was just like a big kid. His enthusiasm was contagious."

Jennifer noted that Jarrett looked like Greg's "Mini-Me."

After the two talked for about a half-hour, Jarrett excused himself to go to the restroom. Greg, who obviously was accustomed to doing things on a whim, asked Jennifer if she thought Jarrett would like to go on a tour of The White House.

"I said *we'd* love to go," Jennifer said.

Greg had a college friend who worked in the mailroom at The White House and had arranged for him to visit the next afternoon. He said he'd make a call and see if he could bring another guest.

The next morning, the Mynears went to the National Press Club to listen to a panel discussion entitled "The 2000 Elections: Will America Vote?"

Corbin Bernsen, an actor best known for his years on the television drama "L.A. Law," emceed. A camera crew taped the event, which was to be part of a television special about the Jefferson Awards. Bernsen would also narrate that.

To Jarrett, the discussion seemed to go on forever. The attention span of an eleven-year-old boy is only so long. The speakers fascinated Jennifer, but she could tell Jarrett was restless.

As the discussion wound down, Bernsen opened the floor to comments. He wanted to know if those who volunteer for community service are more likely to vote than other Americans. And he asked what could be done to get more young people involved in the political process. Jennifer gasped as she saw her son stand up. He stepped into the aisle and took a microphone.

"Adults need to realize they can't do everything on their own," Jarrett said. "There are a lot of kids who could really help out with community projects if they were just asked. My friends have never said 'no' when someone asked them to help. But they have to be asked.

"If they start seeing that they can make a difference when they're young, then I think they'll realize they can make a difference by voting when they're old enough. Kids are caught up in what's cool and what's not cool. America needs to make it cool to be someone who does community service."

Bernsen asked Jarrett for his name and told him he made a really good point.

"Thanks, Jarrett, for helping us look at this from a young person's point of view," the actor said.

Jennifer breathed a sigh of relief, wondering again where her son got all his courage.

After lunch, Jarrett and Jennifer went to the hotel lobby, geared up for a visit to The White House. Greg and his friend Shani Mott (his guest for the Jefferson Awards ceremonies) were already there, ready to go.

Unfortunately, Greg informed them the Secret Service hadn't granted security clearance for Jennifer to go on such short notice. But Jarrett was allowed to be added to the guest list.

"I guess there's not much background to check on an eleven-year-old boy," Jennifer laughed. "I, however, could've had a long history of problems."

So, the trio headed down Pennsylvania Avenue on foot, promising to tell Jennifer all about it when they got back.

Jennifer decided to spend her time at the Natural History Museum. As she left the hotel, she questioned her judgment just for a moment.

"Here I was sending my son off with two people I didn't even know, trusting their every word. But it seemed like such a great opportunity for him, I didn't want him to miss it."

The visit was just to be to the correspondence area, to see where government workers opened mail, stuffed envelopes and basically worked as gophers for The White House staff.

As the quick visit came to an end, Jarrett had a parting thought.

"Could we meet the president's pets– Buddy the dog and Socks the cat?"

"Most people would never dream of asking such a thing," Greg said. "But Jarrett's mentality is to seize all opportunities. You never know what can happen if you don't ask."

To Greg's surprise, The White House aide told them she'd try to arrange for Jarrett to see the animals. She told them to come back in a couple of hours, demonstrating how difficult it was to deny a sincere request from Jarrett.

Greg was as bold as his new friend.

"We'd like to meet the president, too," he said.

The woman smiled.

"That's not going to happen," she said.

"But," Greg protested, "I've been compared to Forrest Gump and Forrest got to meet the president."

Back home in Chicago, Greg was known by many for his tendency to walk into unlikely circumstances, just like the movie character.

"You may meet his dog," the woman said. "That's as close as you're going to get."

Two hours later, Jarrett, Greg and Shani started down Pennsylvania Avenue again for their second trip to the executive mansion. But they had to swing by a designated location to meet up with a fourth guest–Corbin Bernsen.

They had run into the actor on a D.C. sidewalk after the first White House visit and invited him to go, too. He had some free time and readily accepted.

"Apparently, they had no trouble getting *him* clearance," Jennifer said, feigning jealousy. "They must already have records on well-known people."

Off they went–the actor, the teacher and the cancer patient–walking toward the home of the President of the United States.

As the group made its way to The White House, Jarrett overheard several women on the street giggling and whispering.

"That's Corbin Bernsen." Or "Isn't that the guy from L.A. Law?"

The actor walked on, pretending not to hear.

"We teased him about his fans," Jarrett said. "I told him the women were really looking at us."

When they got to their destination, the presidential dog walker was waiting for them, with Buddy and Socks at his side.

Bill Clinton's famous first dog sniffed the visitors and Jarrett stooped to scratch his head. So did Greg. But as he knelt, he stepped on Buddy's tail. The chocolate Labrador retriever gave a quick yelp and Greg jumped back, horrified at the faux pas. Jarrett snickered and told Greg to be careful.

"You're going to get us thrown out of here," he said.

Jarrett gave the cat a quick pat too, but it was Buddy who really interested him.

The dog seemed agitated. An aide suggested it may be a good idea to take Buddy for a walk to settle him down.

"Could we do it?" Jarrett asked, excitedly.

Again, Greg was taken aback by his new friend's boldness.

"Jarrett just never acted like he was asking anything unreasonable. Position or protocol didn't impress him. He was just a kid with a 'why not?' attitude. He's not deterred by his age or that he may be physically tired because of his condition. He literally jumps at chances that come his way."

Over the months that followed, Greg got to know Jarrett better.

"Jarrett is a kid who puts on a strong face when he's around people," Greg said. "If he sits in his room and cries sometimes, no one ever sees it. He has a karma about him that says he can deal with anything. What kind of kid would ask to walk the president's dog? The same kind of kid who thinks he's going to live forever."

The trainer handed the boy the leash. Five people filed behind Jarrett and Buddy–Greg and his friend; two White House aides; and Corbin Bernsen. They walked down a long hallway. Actually, the dog walked Jarrett.

The entourage strolled through several sections of the historic building. Jarrett and Company saw the rooms the public can see on tours, but they also got a more behind-the-scenes look.

They went into the press briefing room, which Jarrett noted looks a lot bigger on TV. He stood behind the same podium the president uses.

Then they went into a kitchen area, used exclusively for preparing floral arrangements.

The size of the room fascinated Jarrett, with its sinks and counters, and a huge selection of vases, pots and utensils that lined the walls. The White House florist showed him a freezer room full of fresh flowers and told him how the arrangements were changed every day.

"It seemed more like what you'd expect in a hotel," Jarrett said. "It was hard to believe all of this was for a house where just one family lived."

Then, the group moved on through a maze of hallways, not really sure where the guides were taking them. An aide told them they had to steer clear of the Oval Office, but she did direct them through the west wing.

As they rounded a corner, a Secret Service agent appeared.

"Step to the right side of the hall," he ordered.

The entourage stopped and backed against the wall.

A large set of double doors opened and out walked President Clinton with the president of Argentina.

Jarrett's mouth fell open. So did Greg's.

Greg reached in his pocket to pull out his camera. The White House aide shook her head and mouthed "no pictures." Greg put his hands back to his side and shrugged his shoulders as if to say "you can't blame me for trying."

The president stopped walking, looked at Jarrett and smiled.

"That dog looks familiar," he said.

"It should," Jarrett replied loudly. "It's your dog!"

Everybody laughed and Greg said, "We're taking good care of him, Mr. President." He was afraid Jarrett would tell the president he stepped on Buddy's tail.

"I just gave him a 'be quiet' look and he got the hint," Greg said.

Mr. Clinton laughed, thanked Jarrett for giving his dog some exercise, shook his hand and continued down the hall. Corbin smiled, remaining unnoticed in the background.

The two world leaders walked outside onto the west wing's portico so dozens of photographers on the lawn could take pictures from a distance.

And thus ended Jarrett's brush with the most powerful politician in the world.

The White House aide rolled her eyes at Greg and said, "You really are Forrest Gump."

When the group came back to the hotel, Jennifer could tell immediately that Greg and Jarrett were especially excited.

"Guess what, Mom," Jarrett said. "We met the president!"

Jennifer looked at Greg, who shook his head in confirmation.

"I thought they were pulling my leg," Jennifer said, "just trying to make me jealous because I didn't get to go along."

They were running late and everyone had to immediately jump on a bus for the next Jefferson Awards event.

"Greg and Jarrett were telling everyone on the bus about running into Bill Clinton, so then I knew it was true," Jennifer said.

She asked Jarrett to tell her all about it.

"I got to walk Buddy," Jarrett said. "He's a really nice dog."

Jarrett and friend Greg Siegman in the west wing of The White House, along with first dog, Buddy Clinton

33
Holding Court

After The White House experience, it was time to get back to business. Five local recipients of the Jefferson Award would receive yet another honor–the Jacqueline Kennedy Onassis Award for Greatest Public Service Benefiting Local Communities. They would be named at a banquet that night in the rotunda of the National Women in Arts Museum.

It was the fanciest dinner Jarrett had ever attended. All of the waiters wore tuxedos. The rotunda was bathed in candlelight and giant floral arrangements adorned each table. Each place setting contained the finest china and crystal wine glasses. Jarrett couldn't imagine why anyone needed that many forks, spoons and knives.

There was one other small boy among the local winners–seven-year-old Trevor DeRuise, whose project was called "Lucky Ladybugs for Lupus." He had raised money for Lupus research by selling rocks painted to look like ladybugs. He and his mother were seated at the same table as Jarrett and Jennifer, along with a staffer from the Supreme Court and board members of the Smithsonian Institution and the American Institute for Public Service.

"Jarrett was starving," Jennifer said. "After all the running around at The White House, he didn't have time to get lunch. So he was really looking forward to the dinner."

But the menu wasn't designed for kids. The waiters stopped at their table with a large tray of meat lined with vegetables.

"I tried to pass it off as pork tenderloin and gravy, but I knew Jarrett wasn't going to like it," Jennifer said.

He took one bite and said he didn't like the texture.

"What is this, really?"

Jennifer told him it was duck.

The other boy at the table immediately began to shake. Images of Donald and Daffy ran through his head.

"I can't eat a duck," Trevor whispered.

"Me neither," said Jarrett.

"But Jarrett," Jennifer said, "you have to eat. You haven't had

148

anything all day. It's not that bad."

In fact, she thought it was fantastic.

The others at the table also tried to convince the boys how good it was, but it was clear they weren't going to budge. To them, ducks were meant for feeding in ponds and laughing at in cartoons.

Trevor's mother whispered to Jennifer that there was a McDonald's across the street. She said she'd slip out and get them Happy Meals. She said she'd save them in her purse and they could eat them later at the hotel. Jennifer nodded her approval.

"I did get Jarrett to eat the mashed potatoes," she said. "But as the night wore on, I could tell both boys were getting weak from hunger."

Finally, she decided there was no need to put on airs. She told the other mother just to go ahead and give the boys the Happy Meals right there at the table. There was no telling how late it would be when they got back to the hotel.

"It ended up being quite the topic of conversation," Jennifer laughed. "Many people came up to the table to talk to us and all of them commented on the Happy Meals."

Many pictures were taken of the two boys sitting there in their suits, with tiny hamburgers laid out on fine china and cold fries spilled across a white tablecloth.

Jarrett was not named as one of the five national winners that night. He hadn't expected to be. But that didn't mean his role in the event was finished.

Sam Beard, the co-founder and president of the American Institute for Public Service, asked Jarrett to come to the final ceremony anyway. The five winners would be honored at the U.S. Supreme Court Building on the last morning. Mr. Beard wanted Jarrett to make a speech too, giving a child's perspective on what it means to be a volunteer. He had been impressed with the way Jarrett had handled interviews and the way he spoke up at the panel discussion.

That night, Jennifer tried to get Jarrett to write a speech in his hotel room. But he was tired.

"Don't worry, Mom," he told her. "I've been thinking about what to say. I have it inside my head."

That's exactly what worried her.

The next day, they showed up at the highest courthouse in the land. The ceremony took place in a conference area just off the main courtroom. A few minutes before it began, the Mynears were seated in the front row, facing a table of dignitaries. Jarrett immediately noticed Senator Glenn and waved at him. He was sure the former astronaut remembered him from his visit to D.C. a month earlier.

He must have because he made eye contact with his wife, who was standing along a side wall, and nodded toward Jarrett. Annie Glenn came over and gave Jarrett a big hug and told him how good it was to see him again.

Then, William Bennett, the nation's former education secretary, came over to introduce himself. Next, a couple of well-known senators walked through the room. Jennifer told Jarrett who they were and then pointed out Justice Sandra Day O'Connor.

"I tried to tell Jarrett how important all these people in the room were," she said. "But he wasn't really phased. He's never thought of one person being any more important than another. To him, everyone is the same."

The ceremony was another one that ran longer than the organizers intended. It followed the formal rules of order where each presenter got multiple introductions. Jennifer thought they might nix Jarrett's speech in the interest of time.

But Sam Beard got up and nodded to Jarrett, indicating he'd be next.

"This is when I usually make some closing remarks," Mr. Beard said. "But today, I want to give my time to someone very special whom I've asked to take my place. I'd like you to meet Jarrett Mynear."

Jarrett walked up to the podium, which bore the seal of the Supreme Court of the United States. His head couldn't be seen above it. Mr. Beard turned a chair around and lifted Jarrett up on it, so he could speak into the microphone.

There was something very moving about the scene. Even before he spoke a word, Jennifer began to cry. She scanned the head table and noticed Corbin Bernsen wiping away tears as well.

It was like years of memories were coming back to Jennifer at this one instant. She thought about all Jarrett had been through and how far he'd come. So many times, she had feared he'd never live to see another day. Now, she could see clearly that God had a purpose for him. He had been allowed to live for a reason. He was a survivor who had gained an audience with some of the most influential people in the nation and he had something to say that they needed to hear. Sometimes, she thought, adults really do need a little child to lead them.

Because Jarrett wouldn't share his speech with her beforehand, she wondered if he'd say something that would make her want to crawl under the table. Instead, she said it was the best speech he'd ever given. It came from the heart. The words tumbled from his mouth like marbles from a jar in an eloquence that seemed magical.

"Kids can do great things," Jarrett began. "They just need to be given support.

"People ask me why I started giving toys out to sick children in the hospital. It's because some adults did the same thing for me. I thought it was so nice that I wanted to do it too. It made me feel better. It took my mind off my sickness. It kept me from feeling sorry for myself.

"Adults need to set a good example and kids will take notice. Kids have good ideas but adults have to make them happen. I couldn't have my Joy Cart if my parents didn't encourage me and help me get the donations and make the deliveries. A lot of adults got behind it and gave me money and toys. They never made me feel like it was a silly idea. They supported me.

"A lot of kids aren't as lucky as I am. They don't get that kind of support. No one asks them what they think or seems to care.

"The media need to get involved too. They need to show the good things kids are doing. We need to have more stories on the news that support kids and give them a chance. We hear a lot about the bad kids who take guns to school or do drugs, but we don't see that much about the ones who help collect toys or food or do nice things for people.

"We're the generation that's going to take over, but we need your help. Show us that there's nothing uncool about helping other people. Not everybody has to do something as big as my Joy Cart. But everybody can do something. Little things can make a big difference. I think that's the message we have to get out. It's not important what you do as long as you do something."

With that, Jarrett turned to Mr. Beard, indicating he was ready to be lifted from the chair. The audience members sat quiet for a moment, stunned at the impact of the short speech they'd just heard. Again, Jennifer noticed a lot of teary eyes.

Then the applause came. And the little man who couldn't see over the podium seemed like a giant.

Jarrett addresses dignitaries at the US Supreme Court
building, June 13, 2000

34
The Banquet and the Bishop

Among the many awards and trophies that line Jarrett's shelves, one of the most beautiful and meaningful is a crystal Madonna–the Queen of Heaven statuette.

Parishioners at the family's church, Mary Queen of the Holy Rosary, nominated Jarrett for the Bishop's Award, one of five honors to be given out at the annual Eastern Kentucky Diocesan Recognition Banquet in 2000.

It was no surprise to those who nominated him when the word came that Jarrett had won.

"This award really meant a lot to us," Jennifer said. "It said that Jarrett was being a Christian witness to others."

Jarrett was all smiles at the awards banquet, looking sharp in his suit and tie. This time, he made sure his shirt was tucked in and his shoes were shiny.

When he was able, Jarrett often served as an altar boy at church and he had developed a special bond with a young associate pastor. Father Linh Nguyen, who had grown up in Vietnam, was yet another friend described by many as "a big kid." He and Jarrett often got into verbal teasing matches.

At the banquet, in the main hall of a Lexington hotel, Jarrett was the only child among 600 adults. The many people who came over to his table to congratulate him made him feel good, but he had his eye on Father Nguyen, who was working the room like a used car salesman, stopping at every table. Jarrett made a mental note to add a couple of lines to his acceptance speech.

When the program began, the lights dimmed and everyone turned their attention to Bishop Kendrick Williams. One by one he called the winners to the podium, telling how their good works exemplified the love of God. The honorees included a medical missionary to Guatemala and a couple who had opened their home to more than twenty foster children.

"They were truly holy people who lived by the Bible every day," Jennifer said.

After a couple of hours, it finally came time to present Jarrett his award. A slide presentation played out, showing Jarrett at home with his family and at the children's hospital pushing The Joy Cart.

When the lights came back up, Jarrett stepped up to the microphone to the thunderous applause he had become accustomed to. He accepted the award, shook the Bishop's hand and posed for a photograph.

And then, his mother said, he decided to do a standup routine.

"As long as I'm up here, I have a few things I want to take care of," Jarrett said.

Oh no, thought Jennifer. She wondered where her son's speech was headed.

"Please, Jarrett," she said to herself. "These are church people. This is a pious occasion. Don't get silly."

But Jarrett wanted to roast his friend in the priesthood.

"Do you know what it's like trying to serve mass with Father Linh?" Jarrett asked the crowd. "He makes these little twitches with his head, left and right, and I can never figure out what he wants me to do."

Those in the crowd from Jarrett's parish laughed. They were familiar with Nguyen's mannerisms.

"And people worry about my health, but they should worry about Father Linh. Did you see how he was going from table to table tonight, toasting everybody with wine? He must've put away quite a few bottles. I'm worried about *his* health."

The Father shook his finger at Jarrett and smiled. The crowd roared.

Then Jarrett thanked his parents and other family members for all they had done to support his project. He asked them to stand from their table in the right corner of the room.

"If you get a blinding glare from over there, that's my Granny Jeanne. She always has sequins on."

Again, the crowd laughed. Jarrett's grandmother was mortified. She didn't think he was giving the proper acceptance speech for such a highly religious ceremony.

Jennifer worried about that too, until the benediction was delivered and people started to move toward the door.

"Many people came over and thanked Jarrett for lightening the mood," she said. "And the Bishop had laughed as loudly as anyone. So, I guess it was OK. Maybe Jarrett had sat through too many solemn speeches that night and just had to burn up some energy."

No matter what the occasion, Jarrett always seemed to steal the show. And his family believed the axiom that laughter is good medicine. Plus, he couldn't wait to go to church again. Maybe he just wanted to get more material to use against Father Linh. But, whatever his motivation, his mother knew that church was good for him.

35
Oprah

Over the years, Jarrett had impressed more and more journalists with his gentle spirit, his speaking abilities and his quotable quotes. He was a good story; there was no doubt about it.

One reporter who never forgot the young man was Melinda Morrison, who had interviewed him while working at WHAS-TV in Louisville.

"Melinda kept up with us through e-mail," Jennifer said. "She wasn't like so many reporters who pass through your life once and you never see them again. She checked in often to get an update on Jarrett's condition."

My co-anchor at WDKY developed the same kind of relationship. Jennifer Nime understood Melinda's affection. "Jarrett is just one of those people you can't get out of your mind once you meet him," she said.

My on-air partner, who is single, often found that Jarrett was a good Saturday night date. She took him to movies and to dinner many times. I teased her about "liking them young."

No doubt, Melinda would've done the same thing had she lived closer. By the beginning of 2000, she had moved back to her native Seattle to do freelance work. Part of her work included producing segments for talk show queen Oprah Winfrey.

Melinda worked for months to try to convince the Oprah producers to do a segment about Jarrett.

"I fell in love with the kid the first time I met him," Melinda said. "He was magic. I saw him healing kids as he went room to room with his Joy Cart–not curing them, but healing their broken spirits."

In November, the time was right. The show was a few months into a project called "Remembering Your Spirit," a series of videotaped reports about people who were making a difference in the world. It included stories about people who overcame all sorts of obstacles from discrimination to medical hardships and incredible financial burdens.

Melinda pitched the story to producers in Chicago when they

called her looking for ideas for a segment on medical miracles.

"I had one day to get on a plane and get to Kentucky," she said. "I called Jarrett's mother and apologized for the short notice. But I was determined to get there and get it done."

She contracted with a production crew from Cincinnati and showed up at UK Children's Hospital Nov. 3, 2000.

Melinda scoped out the hospital and made small talk with the Mynears and hospital public relations staff as she waited for the crew to arrive. More than an hour passed and she began to get stressed. It was a Friday afternoon. Many of the children were about to be released for the weekend. She wanted to get a lot of video of Jarrett passing out toys, but if the crew didn't hurry up, there wouldn't be many kids to put on camera. Melinda wanted this story to be just right and it was off to a bad start.

At last, the crew pulled into the hospital's loading zone. The driver apologized, telling Melinda how he'd gotten lost.

But she barely heard the words. She rushed the freelancers to the hospital's playroom and supervised while they set up lights, tested camera angles and did microphone checks.

When it seemed everything was working, Melinda called Jennifer and Jarrett in to do an interview.

Just as she asked the first questions, the sound of jackhammers pierced the air. The hospital was in the middle of a major renovation.

"Stop!" Melinda shouted frantically. "We can't do the interview with all that noise in the background."

When the racket died down, Melinda asked her first questions and, as she put it, Jarrett gave phenomenal answers. But before he could complete his thoughts, the hammering began again.

"Jarrett would give me a perfect sound bite and I'd have to do it over and over," she said. Frustration got the best of her.

She excused herself and went to find the hospital's public relations person. That set off a chain of events that took another hour to resolve. The university had to make a series of calls to get the construction crews to stop for a few minutes. Time is money and it's no easy task to inject a manmade (or in this case, womanmade) delay into the work schedule of state-paid contractors.

"By that time, I was begging parents to hold their kids there for a little while longer," she said. "Most of them understood that it was a big deal to be on Oprah so they were quite nice about it."

As she was about to wave the white flag of surrender, the jackhammers fell silent.

Later, everyone at the hospital would joke about how only Jarrett could bring construction to a halt. Sick people had to listen to the noise every day and would've no doubt loved to have pulled the plug on the ruckus many times, but only this eleven-year-old boy had actually been able to do it.

Melinda conducted a poignant interview. She still remembers the last thing Jarrett said while the camera rolled.

"I don't know how much longer I'll be here," he said, without a hint of drama. "But I hope the kids will remember that I did something nice for them and they'll do something kind for someone in their life."

Tears welled up in Melinda's eyes. It was like she'd been hit by one of those jackhammers on the other side of the wall. She turned and looked at the cameraman, who was also dabbing the corner of his eyes.

When the story aired exactly a week later, no one could've known it was a rush job. It was beautifully done and, despite all the chaos, Jarrett's personality shone through.

Melinda didn't see the show and she knew Oprah wouldn't see the segment until it played in front of her on live TV. She was in an airport as the show ended. Her cell phone rang and a producer in Chicago said simply, "You made the boss cry."

As the show went off the air, the last thing viewers saw was Jarrett's smiling face. The closing credits included his e-mail address.

Melinda decided after the show that she wanted to help Jarrett's dream of expansion come true. So many people had talked about forming their own Joy Carts, but none had gotten off the ground on a regular schedule.

"I just couldn't get it out of my mind," she said. "I knew this was something I could do. I had the complete power to do what Jarrett was asking."

Within days, she presented a business proposal to the Seattle Children's Hospital–an idea it accepted immediately.

"Melinda called us now and again and said, 'I'm serious about this. I want to do it here in Seattle,'" Jennifer said. "We thought that was a nice idea, but we really didn't put much stock in it. We knew how busy she was."

They soon learned they had underestimated the wrong person.

36
"You've Got Mail"

The phone rang at the Mynear household all evening after the taped piece ran on Oprah. Just as with the Rosie O'Donnell appearances, friends and relatives wanted to call to congratulate Jarrett on his performance. No one in the family got around to checking their e-mail that night.

But the next day, when Jennifer logged on to her AOL account, the familiar digitized voice informed her: "You've Got Mail."

Boy, did she ever. The page was full and as she scrolled down, it just seemed to go on and on. Hundreds of messages filled the in-box. She didn't recognize the account names of the senders. They were all Oprah viewers who had jotted down the address as the show went off the air.

She called Jarrett into the room so he could see the instantaneous response.

"Oh my gosh, Mom," Jarrett said. "How are we going to read all that?"

After they looked at the first five or six messages, they made a decision.

"We have to respond to these," Jennifer said. "All of them. These people were nice enough to say these things, we can't ignore them."

She thought they'd take just a few at a time. They crafted a form letter of sorts to send en mass, but it became apparent that wasn't always the appropriate response.

"Many of the writers had specific questions and quite a few of them wanted to know how they could start their own toy carts," Jennifer said. "And many of them wanted to know more about Jarrett's cancer, saying they had a child or a relative who had just been diagnosed with Ewing's and were at a loss for information."

For the rest of the week, Doug, Jennifer and Jarrett all spent time answering the e-mail. But the new messages were coming in faster than they could clear the old ones. When the count reached 1,500, the family decided it needed help.

Jennifer mentioned the volume of response to Ginger Williams,

Jarrett's computer lab instructor. Jarrett was one of the star pupils in STLP, the Student Technology Leadership Program. The group was made up of several students who were junior computer wizards. These kids set up networks within the school and taught other students how to use the advanced functions on the computers. The sixth, seventh and eighth graders were often called to troubleshoot problems for teachers in the classroom.

Jarrett had been interested in computers since he was eighteen months old. Long before he reached school age, he would sit in Doug's lap and they'd play games, write programs and surf the web together.

"Jarrett definitely got that from his dad," Jennifer said. "I can't do much beyond the basics."

Jarrett's lab instructor suggested working the Oprah responses into the curriculum for the STLP students. The Mynears were glad to take her up on the offer.

The Mynears forwarded the e-mail to the school's computer lab and the students took the challenge to respond to the letters and ran with it. They set up address books, wrote several reply letters to fit different situations and even cross-referenced responses. For example, if three people in central Ohio expressed an interest in starting a toy cart, the students got them in contact with each other.

"It was a tremendous help to us," Jennifer said. "Of course, when they agreed to do it, I'm not sure they realized the letters would keep coming."

Hundreds more letters were forwarded from Oprah staff members– letters that had gone to them instead of directly to the Mynears.

"I want to emphasize that we read every e-mail," Jennifer said. "We just let the students help respond. People have a right to know their letters got to us. When they were of a more personal nature, I responded personally."

Jarrett had hundreds of the letters printed and he kept them in binders. If he ever had doubts about the impact of his project, they vanished when he read the mail:

What an awesome young man you are! I am a mother of three. I live in a small town in Texas. I feel pretty confident we could get the donations for this but my question to you is this: Could we name our cart after you?

****

I am a 34 yr. old wife and mother and just want to tell you that God is so very proud of you. Your life is a wonderful example of how we all should live.

****

Hey there, we think you are the best. Because of you we are looking into starting a joy cart ourselves here in Florida. We honor your spirit!!

****

I am 24 years old and I live alone in a single bedroom apartment in Edmonton, Alberta, Canada. I don't have very much but I have decided to help you. I thought at first I would send money, but I don't think that would be enough. Instead, I will help the kids that are here. Maybe a teddy bear given to a child will help them fight.

****

I have been feeling sorry for myself because I have been laid off for over 2.5 months. When I saw your story today I was just laying in bed. When I listened to you speak, hearing your sensitivity and wisdom brought me to tears.

On Monday when the various business offices open, I am going to check into starting a toy cart or at least volunteering my time at the local children's hospital. I feel like you have given this 38-year-old person a new lease on life.

****

My heart swelled to see today's Oprah show. I am sending $100 and hope that you can make a few children smile. I also intend to inquire as to whether there is an opportunity to have a Jarrett's cart in our local hospital here in New Jersey.

****

Have you ever considered that you are a role model for several adults? Well, it's true. Thanks for warming my heart.

****

Hi there Jarrett--
Today I saw you on Oprah. Your outlook and kindness made me cry. Even my 6-year-old little boy said "wow, what a nice kid." Keep up the great work!

****

I consider myself your #1 fan, and even though I only saw you on TV a few minutes ago, you are my favorite person in the world besides my family, of course.

****

Hey Jarrett: Don't know if you remember me, but I was with you the day we all visited the White House, met Buddy and got pushed aside as President Clinton strolled by. My whole company decided to dedicate this day to you and together focus our energies on your speedy recovery. One of the guys even asked (after I told him how cool you were) if we could put you in one of our movies. Let's just say the vote was a big unanimous YES!

So get better soon. We'll get you out here and put that smile of yours in front of the camera!

Your buddy (not the dog)
Corbin Bernsen

The ways people thought of to help astounded the Mynears. Several families made it their Christmas project to put extra gifts around the tree marked for "Jarrett's Joy Cart."

ACE Insurance Company in their town of Nicholasville organized a "poker run" in which nearly a hundred motorcyclists traveled to several checkpoints, picking up a different playing card at each stop. At the end of the ride, the best hand won a prize. Jarrett strapped on a helmet and rode on the back of a Suzuki with one of the organizers. All of the proceeds went to The Joy Cart.

The local Goody's department store sponsored a car show in its parking lot. Entry fees went to the project.

Insight Communications, the Lexington cable company, offered free installation for a month to any customer who would donate a new toy or ten dollars to The Joy Cart. It took in $8,000 and 400 toys.

And the Lexington Rotary Club invited the Mynears to a meeting, saying the endowment committee wanted to make a donation. The family expected maybe a few hundred dollars. Jarrett about fell over when the committee president handed him an oversized check for $20,000. The symbolic check represented the club's pledge to allocate money for years to come.

One Nicholasville family donated more than 600 beanie babies. Clarence Rogers had bought, sold and collected the squeezable stuffed animals for years.

"The hobby had gotten out of hand," Rogers told a local newspaper reporter. Hundreds of the toys were left over from McDonald's Happy Meal boxes. Rogers said the family's two German shepherds helped eat a lot of hamburgers when the collection was being built up. "When we heard about The Joy Cart, we knew exactly what to do with the toys. Children at the hospital will enjoy them more than we do."

That was the first time Jarrett could count dogs among his growing list of donors.

37
A Ton of Bricks

During the fall of 2000, Jarrett was fitted with a new prosthesis–his fourth. It took him a month or so to feel comfortable with it as he adjusted to the new length and the minor differences in the tension and flexibility in the knee joint.

He began to complain off and on that October about back pain and soreness in his hip, but his parents believed that was still just part of getting used to the new leg. They had been told to expect some soreness for quite a while as Jarrett's spine adjusted to his new stance.

"I also noticed he was beginning to lose weight again," Jennifer said. "But appetite had always been as issue with Jarrett. It was something that came and went."

Still, as they went to the hospital in November for Jarrett's next scheduled round of bone scans, Jennifer had a bad feeling. Things had been going better than they probably had a right to expect them to for a long time. It had been more than two years since his bone marrow transplant. His spirit had been buoyed by the Oprah exposure just a few days before.

"There were no glaring red flags as we went to the hospital that day," she said. "Again, it was just part of the routine."

Her good friend Kathy Tabb went too, planning to join them for a nice lunch once the tests were completed.

Jarrett went in for a CT scan first.

"The technicians have always been wonderful," Jennifer said. "They would chitchat and joke around and make us feel at ease."

But this day was different. The technicians seemed especially quiet when they did the scans. They'd whisper from time to time, obviously trying to keep their voices low enough so Jennifer couldn't hear.

"They had never avoided me before, but I could tell they knew something was wrong."

She didn't confront them then, but she began to feel sick to her stomach. Her strong intuition told her she'd better brace herself for

166

bad news. Other mothers may have demanded that the technicians stop whispering and tell them what they were seeing on their monitors, but Jennifer wasn't in any hurry to hear what had them concerned. She kept watching for some sign of hope–a smile, relaxed facial muscles, a freeing sigh–anything that could indicate her fears were unfounded.

The scans were taken away for a doctor to read.

"He always made it a point to talk to Jarrett when we went in for tests," Jennifer said. "But that day, he made himself scarce. I asked when he would come in to see us and they kept telling me he was too busy; he had no time to talk."

Jennifer looked at Kathy and told her she was getting bad vibes. Kathy tried to reassure Jennifer that it was too early to be worried. She fibbed when she said she didn't get the impression the technicians were avoiding them.

"They're just busier than usual today," Kathy said. But deep down, she had the same gut feeling that bad news was brewing.

Then, the staffers took Jarrett to a different department for a bone scan.

"I got the same evasive looks and when I asked how it was going, I got vague answers," Jennifer said.

Time crept, but eventually a nurse called Jennifer into the hall and told her Dr. Gary Conrad wanted to talk to her about Jarrett's bone scan. The walk to the doctor's station seemed like a trip to the gallows.

Dr. Conrad had a grim look on his face as he got straight to the point. He told Jennifer cancer had invaded Jarrett's skeleton in the spine and pelvis, among other areas.

"I won't lie to you," the doctor said. "It's bad. You may want to get Doug here."

Once again, Jennifer felt as though she'd been hit by the proverbial ton of bricks, with a force as strong as the one she absorbed the first time she was told her baby had cancer at age two-and-a-half.

"It was probably even worse this time," Jennifer said. "The first time, there was naivety on our part. Now, I really knew what he could be facing."

A technician took her into a private office so she could call her husband. She broke down in tears and had trouble composing her thoughts as she punched in Doug's phone number.

Outside the office, Kathy cried and several of the nurses and technicians mopped their own tears. It seemed that entire wing of the hospital was cloaked in sadness as the word spread. None of the nurses knew what to do to make it better. If it would've helped to throw a chair or let out a chorus of primal screams, they'd have done it. Jarrett was everybody's little pal and now it appeared their favorite patient was "too far gone." Maybe they were feeling as sorry for themselves as they were for him. They couldn't imagine not having Jarrett around anymore.

When Doug arrived, Chief Pediatric Oncologist Dr. Jeffrey Moscow joined them to discuss the CT scan. It showed at least twelve small tumors on Jarrett's liver and a softball-sized tumor that clung to the right side of his abdomen. They could see how the largest tumor was squeezing Jarrett's stomach outward.

Jarrett had lost more weight than his parents realized. The swollen stomach had fooled them.

"Basically, he had no stomach left," Jennifer said. "It was almost all tumor. The doctors couldn't understand how he had been eating at all."

The tumors had seemed to come so suddenly. A check back at a bone scan three months earlier did show some dark marks on the spine. That had been attributed to the "wear and tear" of Jarrett's shifting posture as he adjusted to his new leg.

The doctors did a biopsy to confirm whether this was another case of Ewing's sarcoma. It was. The disease proved once again how malicious it can be. It had stayed dormant and hidden for four years, but it refused to go away for good.

38
Something to Say

The bad news couldn't keep Jarrett from his next public appearance. If anything, it made him more determined to find an audience.

He had been asked to join the Kentucky delegation on the President's Cancer Panel, a conference organized by the National Cancer Institute. The institute set up a series of meetings around the country to gather information to be presented to the president and members of Congress.

Jarrett was the youngest child ever asked to participate. The meeting in Nashville would include presentations from health care professionals in eight southern states, Puerto Rico and the U.S. Virgin Islands.

It was scheduled for November 16th and 17th, just a week after the devastating diagnosis.

"I thought about calling the Kentucky leader and telling them to get another representative," Jennifer said. "But Jarrett insisted on going. He had done his homework. He had interviewed Dr. Moscow. He felt he had something to say that the president needed to hear."

Jarrett was concerned that if he didn't go, there would be no children on the panel. And he truly believed children should have a voice.

The topic was equity in insurance coverage. Jarrett found out from Dr. Moscow that a lot of the children at the UK Hospital were on Medicaid. Many of them received more than one type of chemotherapy per day but Medicaid would only pay for one daily treatment.

Jennifer helped Jarrett write his speech, using her son's notes.

The second day of the conference at Vanderbilt University was Kentucky's day to make a presentation. The delegation would get one hour to speak that morning. Jarrett sat on the dais with four other guests, including the director of the Markey Cancer Center and a colorectal surgeon from Louisville.

Each of the four spoke ahead of Jarrett. The woman who

169

addressed the panel just before Jarrett's turn talked about getting malignant melanoma in October 1986, breast cancer in her left side in October 1994 and breast cancer on the right in October 1996.

"So, you see, I don't like the month of October at all," she said.

When Jarrett was introduced, the panel's chairman set a microphone at the table for him. He was too small to go to the podium.

He began, as usual, looking totally relaxed.

"Like Ms. Farris was saying, her bad month is October. Mine is September," he began. "Three of my diagnoses have been in September, all around the same date."

That wasn't on the script.

Jennifer became nervous. She didn't want him to ad-lib. From her seat in the audience, she began waving a copy of his speech, pointing at it frantically.

Jarrett nodded his acknowledgement and began to read his prepared remarks.

Jennifer sat back, breathing easier. Doug patted her hand, indicating things would be OK.

Jarrett told the audience how he had just been re-diagnosed a week ago and how he was prepared to go another round with cancer.

"Even though I'm not feeling well, it's important for me that you hear about my concern for the cancer patients of Kentucky, especially the children.

"As you can imagine, my family and I have met hundreds of pediatric patients over the years. And one of the most important things we've learned is that to get through this you have to have a good system to meet *all* the needs of the patients and their families, not just the medical ones.

"Many of the families would be better able to cope with the diagnoses, treatments and all the other things that follow if they had a good psychological support system. We have seen families break apart because of the stress of long hospitalizations and the uncertainty of their children's illnesses.

"Families with private insurance rarely find that coverage is offered for services to help them learn to cope with the stresses cancer brings into a family, especially one where there are siblings. For those in Kentucky with public insurance, these services are typically not available either.

"Cancer not only brings health worries, but it brings financial pressures and emotional stresses as well. I know, firsthand, the importance of having a positive, healthy attitude and knowing that my family is beside me all the way."

Jarrett went on to address the Medicaid issue and the fact that multiple daily chemo treatments were not covered.

"Medicaid only pays for one of those treatments. The rest are given, as they should be, but payment comes from the pool of money used to run and staff the Pediatric Oncology Department.

"Our hospital doesn't have enough nurses or doctors because the money is being used to cover chemotherapy and its administration, as well as other procedures, since Kentucky's Medicaid doesn't. This means the pediatric patients suffer because of low staffing."

Then Jarrett eloquently told the panel about his late friend, C.B. Wolford. Jarrett said there was a real problem with a delay of diagnoses for children who lived in rural areas.

"C.B. didn't even have a fighting chance to battle his cancer because doctors at home kept telling his parents that he was having growing pains and was just getting lazy when he complained of being very sore and very tired. A CT scan clearly showed a large tumor in his lung, but it was not identified at that time. The doctor who dealt with C.B. told his mother that he was probably developing breast tissue due to puberty. He said that he had a little more than most boys, but he would be fine.

"*Where* you live in a state shouldn't be a factor in how quickly you are diagnosed and provided with cutting-edge treatment and choices."

As he was about to close, Jarrett looked up from his script.

"Mom, if you're taking a picture, the shutter is closed."

Jennifer pulled the camera away from her face and just shook her head. But she looked at the shutter and he was right. The audience laughed. Jennifer's face turned red.

Then he wrapped things up, not immodestly, by saying, "I'm a hard act to follow. I guess that's why they put me at the end of the line."

There wasn't a speaker on the program who would deny it, as the audience responded with a standing ovation.

39
Downhill

In the days that followed, Dr. Moscow talked to the Mynears about a clinical trial for immuno-therapy that was starting at the National Institute for Health (NIH). That would mean a series of vaccines. He told them, "It may be too late for conventional treatment. This may be Jarrett's only glimmer of hope."

So, in mid-December, the family went once again to yet another unfamiliar hospital, the institute in Bethesda, Maryland. If it was grasping at straws, so be it. Give them a handful. "Giving up" was a phrase that had long ago been wiped out of their vocabulary.

In the week before they made the trip, Jarrett's condition deteriorated rapidly. The pain in his spine and abdomen grew much worse and he took large amounts of pain medication. He stopped wearing his prosthesis and stayed in a wheelchair most of his waking hours.

"The Ewing's came in bursts," his mother said. "It broke through two vertebrae in his neck. He couldn't hold his head up as we went into a meeting with the protocol chairman at the hospital in Maryland."

The doctors there had Jarrett admitted immediately. They placed him under an around-the-clock neurological watch, concerned he could be paralyzed if there were any more strain on his neck.

The next day, the doctors stood over Jarrett's bed and told his family he'd need twenty more days of radiation on the two main tumor sites on his spine.

"At that point, Jarrett rolled over, curled up into a ball and tuned everybody out," his mother said. "He didn't want to hear that he wasn't going anywhere."

Again, Christmas was just around the corner and the boy couldn't stand the thought of not being home for the holiday.

Another day passed and the radiologists were in disagreement about the safety of moving Jarrett. Some believed they could get him stabilized in a couple of days and allow him to return to Kentucky for the radiation. Others thought he should stay put.

172

Dr. Moscow consulted with the NIH doctors over the telephone and assured them the staff at UK could take care of Jarrett. They agreed on three days of radiation in Maryland, coupled with a dose of steroids to reduce the swelling in the spinal column.

"The doctors at NIH were very methodical," Jennifer said. "They took great care to make sure he could travel. They checked his response to the radiation every day and decided he was OK to fly."

So, on the evening of the third treatment, they bundled their son in a warm jacket and got on a plane home. Jarrett was extremely weak. His family had seen him go downhill rapidly that week.

"We weren't sure if it was stress, fatigue or anxiety," his mother said. "But we knew we had to get his spirits up. Getting home for Christmas was part of that strategy."

Their plane touched down in Louisville late that night and they made the 90-minute drive home. They were due at the UK Children's Hospital at 7:30 a.m. for a radiation treatment.

"We were exhausted," Jennifer said. "But it was worth it to be back home."

The radiation would continue for the next three weeks, five days a week, attacking those two tumor sites on the spine. The tumor on the abdomen was much too large to irradiate. The doctors were still wondering what to do about it. They couldn't just cut it out. They didn't know exactly how it was connected to other organs and an operation could've caused severe bleeding.

They made the traditional Christmas visit to Granny Jeanne's house after opening presents at their Lexington home. All of the relatives came in and everyone tried to act as if nothing had changed.

"But it was very melancholy," Jennifer said. "We had trouble putting on a happy face. We all knew things had never been this bad with Jarrett. He was on so much pain medication he could barely stay awake at times."

The steroids had changed his mood. The young boy who never seemed to get down about his condition now had times when he was short-tempered and withdrawn.

He sat at the holiday dinner table–which was covered with turkey, dressing, vegetables and sweets–and tried to take a bite of his favorite dishes.

"He wanted to eat so badly," Jennifer said. "But he'd take one

173

bite and sit there with tears in his eyes. It made him feel full and bloated."

Physiologically, his circumstances were taking a toll on Jarrett.

In the week that followed, Jennifer suspended all efforts to keep her son current with his schoolwork. He couldn't go to school and she didn't even try to put textbooks or homework in front of him. That was something she had never ignored before.

"He was just too sick to keep his mind on anything," she said. "Some days he would be overdosed and in a stupor."

It upset Jarrett to have those feelings of disorientation. He tried not to take the pain medications because he didn't like the way they made him feel. But pain almost always won out.

Jarrett's liver wasn't clearing the way it should. One tumor blocked his bile duct, causing toxins to back up into his body. At times he couldn't go to the bathroom at all. His throat became constricted, making it almost impossible to swallow. Sometimes he spit up blood or it showed up in his urine. Even though two inches of snow covered the ground outside Jarrett's window, everything looked dark to the Mynears.

When the radiation ended, Dr. Moscow decided to attack the abdominal tumor with a combination of two types of chemotherapy that had worked for Jarrett at separate times. It was a shot in the dark whether the two would enhance each other's effectiveness.

As Dr. Moscow discussed his plan with Jennifer during an office visit, Jarrett began to ask questions. It was clear he needed things laid out in black and white.

"I nodded to Dr. Moscow, indicating it was OK to be straight with Jarrett," his mother said. "We had always been honest with him and he knew things were getting worse every day. There was no need to sugarcoat it for him."

But there's no easy way to tell a child he's probably going to die. Dr. Moscow looked Jarrett straight in the eyes and told him the severity of the situation and how the cancer had invaded his liver, pancreas and skeleton.

"The choices are limited, Jarrett," the doctor said. "As you know, Ewing's is a smart cancer and it may have developed immunity to the chemo we want to use. We just don't know if it will work."

Jarrett dropped his head and tears flowed as if a spigot had been opened. Then Jennifer lost it and Dr. Moscow excused himself.

The boy climbed onto his mother's lap and they held each other in silence.

After several minutes, Jarrett raised his head, wiped his tears with the back of his hand and looked at his mother.

"It's going to be all right," he said. "I've done this before and I can do it again. It's going to be all right.

"It's going to be all right." He repeated it again and he patted his mother on the back.

"I reminded him that parents are the ones who are supposed to keep it together in these situations," Jennifer said, amazed that her son was the one who was doing the consoling.

"I know, Mom, but I'm better at it than you," Jarrett said, forcing a smile.

A couple of the nurses stood at their work station just around the corner, including Anne Hoskins, who had worked at the clinic 25 years and had tended to Jarrett since his first day there. The nurses huddled together and shared the sorrow, as they tried to muffle their crying.

Later, nurse Anne told Jarrett that she felt like kicking the wall when she heard he'd been diagnosed with cancer again.

"Anne," Jarrett replied, "That would just be wasting energy that could be used for something positive."

Anne tried to fill her head with positive thoughts. It wasn't difficult to think of things about Jarrett that made her laugh. She remembered the time he came out of the chemo room with blood all over his face.

"We were all about to faint," Anne said. "It looked like something had gone terribly wrong. Then he started laughing. It was all fake. He had painted himself with something he had gotten out of a Halloween makeup kit."

And she recalled how Jarrett had learned to mimic the noises the IV machines made.

"He could imitate the beeping sounds perfectly," she said. "As soon as a nurse would leave the room, he'd start in—'beep...beep'— and we'd come running, thinking it was time to change the fluids. Everyone else in the room would break out laughing. It would drive

us crazy, running back and forth."

It was that spirit that kept her upbeat about a potentially-depressing job.

Jarrett asked his mother to bring Dr. Moscow back into the room.

"Tell me again what the options are," he asked the doctor.

"We can either take the aggressive route and try to slow the cancer down or we can give you medications to make sure you're comfortable," Moscow said.

"The chemo would be harsh and could make you really sick. To be honest, Jarrett, it could affect your quality of life."

Jarrett looked at Dr. Moscow, squarely and firmly. He made sure there was eye contact.

"You give me the chemo and I'll be fine," he said.

"I'm not going to play games with you," Moscow said. "This is hard-core chemo."

"It's not my time to go," Jarrett replied. "You give me the chemo and I'll take care of the rest of it."

And that was that.

Jarrett went home that day, with skin and eyes yellowed with jaundice, skinny arms and a distended stomach that made him look like one of the starving children you see in drought-ravaged third world countries. But, even in that state, he showed strength.

"After he makes his choices, he moves on," Dr. Moscow said. "I've had many tough conversations with him. But the next thing you'd know, he'd be playing video games. We all wish we could dispatch the great issues in our life with such ease."

When Jarrett showed up to begin the round of chemotherapy, the doctors ordered yet another CT scan. His mother described the image of his stomach as "a squashed file folder." The tumor took up all the space.

For the first few days, the doctors had Jarrett on low doses. He handled it well so they gradually pushed the treatments to full strength. But Jarrett was a long way from the vibrant child he was known to be.

Many of the regular patients at the pediatric clinic refused to go into the treatment room when Jarrett was there.

"It hurt them too badly to see Jarrett in that shape," Jennifer said.

"One boy stayed in the waiting room and got his chemo treatments there."

Each day when Jennifer wheeled Jarrett into the clinic, she made sure not to make eye contact with Anne and some of the other nurses. Just a glance could make them all fall apart and Jarrett didn't need to see more tears.

One day in early February, Kathy Tabb sat with Jarrett as he got his treatment. Jennifer was away on an errand.

He told Kathy he'd like to do something special for his mother for Valentine's Day. Kathy thought about it for a moment and then asked Jarrett if he'd like to paint ceramics.

He thought that was a good idea, so Kathy arranged to take him to The Mad Potter–a shop that lets customers put their own designs on mugs, plates and bowls before they're glazed and fired.

"He was really sick when I took him there. He had been spitting up blood and felt miserable, but he insisted on going ahead with it," Kathy said.

As they scanned the shelves at the store, Jarrett seemed to take forever to pick out something to paint. He was slower than some of the kids who became overwhelmed when they were invited to get something off The Joy Cart.

Finally, he chose a coffee mug.

Kathy and Jarrett sat at the wooden table, with more than a dozen colors of paint opened in front of them. Jarrett moved slowly and carefully, painting hearts and flowers around the sides of the mug.

Then he took a brush and covered the entire palm of his hand with blue paint.

"Jarrett, you're making a mess!" Kathy said. "You're going to get paint all over your mug."

"I know," he said softly.

Then he wrapped his entire hand around the mug and grasped it firmly.

When he pulled his hand away, there was a perfect imprint of his palm and five fingers.

"I want Mom to always be able to hold my hand," he said. "All she'll have to do is pick up this mug and I'll be with her."

Tears welled up in Kathy's eyes. It was heart-wrenching. She couldn't believe he had come up with such a profound idea.

Jennifer had the same reaction when Jarrett presented the gift to her a week later. That multi-colored mug instantly became the most precious piece in the china cabinet.

By the end of February, Jarrett started to eat more solid foods and he began to get out of the wheelchair more. He didn't use the prosthesis much. He accepted being carried.

In mid-March, the doctors did another CT scan and a MRI and both showed some shrinkage of the tumor.

"Not anything tremendous, mind you," said Jennifer. "It was just a matter of millimeters. But it was in the right direction."

Two more weeks passed and they could tell Jarrett was feeling better. The jaundice went away, as did the swelling in his stomach.

As always, his parents were concerned about his emotional well-being. "We had learned that had a lot to do with how he did physically."

So, again they allowed him to accept invitations and to be reintroduced to the active social life to which he had been accustomed.

Terry Hagan often showed up with his pickup truck to take Jarrett to a movie. He'd throw the wheelchair in the back, hoist Jarrett in the cab and off they'd go. Sometimes they'd just go to Terry's house to watch a rented movie on his VCR. Once they took a trip to Fort Knox. As a retired Army reservist, Terry had connections. Jarrett had a grand time climbing over the tanks and sitting in an Apache helicopter.

Three other kids went on the trip too, which turned into a twelve-hour day.

"There wasn't a minute when one of them wasn't talking," Terry remembered. "When we went into the military museum, Jarrett started teaching class–telling the others all about the helmets, the survival kits and the firepower of the weapons. You would have never known he was sick."

Jennifer's brother Christopher organized similar outings, hauling his nephew off on fishing trips, to hockey games and his favorite ice cream parlor.

And several Lexington police officers took Jarrett under their wings as a little brother, often taking him on field trips so he could see their vehicles and crime-fighting tools up close.

"I'd hold my breath every time," Jennifer admitted. She knew Jarrett didn't feel well but he refused to be homebound.

The police department printed thousands of collectible cards which pictured officers children may see in the community–those who worked with dogs or rode bicycles, motorcycles and horses. The idea was to pass them out in schools and on playgrounds to make children feel comfortable around police. An additional trading card showed up in the deck in the spring of 2001. The police made Jarrett an honorary member of the force and featured him on a card.

"It was good for him to have all these distractions," Jennifer said.

The chemo was adding quantity to his life. His parents wanted to be sure there was quality, too.

40
Faith

Robin Silverman says she's spent twenty years looking for the good in people. The inspirational author from Grand Forks, North Dakota collects stories of ordinary people who do remarkable things. It was just a matter of time before she discovered Jarrett.

After a speech for a rotary club in Texas, a man in the audience told Robin about Taryn Pream, a teenager from Thief River Falls, Minnesota. In 1998, Taryn became the victim of Internet harassment. She received disturbing e-mails that said things such as "I am your worst nightmare" and "Your troubles are just beginning." Fear overtook her and her grades slipped dramatically over several weeks as the e-mails kept coming. But the local sheriff's department tracked down the culprit, one of Taryn's classmates, and sentenced him to 100 hours of community service. Had he been an adult, he would've faced jail time.

Taryn turned the negative into a positive, developing brochures and an educational program for other teens to tell them how to use the Internet safely–warning them about stalkers in the chat rooms and the consequences of sending threats through cyberspace.

Robin contacted Taryn, hoping to tell her story in an upcoming book entitled "Something Wonderful is About to Happen." Taryn was glad to tell her story, and she also told Robin she had a friend the author should know about. That friend was Jarrett Mynear, whom Taryn had met as a fellow winner of the Prudential Spirit of Community Awards.

"All I knew about when I picked up the phone was The Joy Cart," Robin said. "But as I talked to Jarrett's mother on the phone, I quickly learned about his latest diagnosis and I felt a sense of urgency and helplessness."

Robin asked Jennifer if she believed in the power of prayer.

"That's always been an important thing to us," Jennifer said. "It gets us through a lot of dark days."

Robin, who had really just begun to know about this family and its complicated journey, felt compelled to write a prayer for Jarrett.

She told Jennifer how her mother-in-law had been given six hours to live, as she lay in a bed comatose and on life-support.

"We were told to gather the family," Robin said. "She wasn't expected to make it through the night."

But as she stood over the bed, the family's rabbi came in and told her how the congregation was praying for her mother-in-law. A few minutes later, a Catholic priest stopped by and said he would be praying. And within the hour, the hospital's Protestant chaplain popped his head into the room to say the same thing.

Robin's mother-in-law made a full recovery and she became convinced it was because of the prayers.

"The doctors were baffled," Robin told Jennifer. "I started to read and research the power of positive prayer and came upon dozens of medical studies that proved it's an effective medicine."

Robin emphasized that she wasn't talking about faith healing or new age hocus-pocus.

"I got my information from scientific studies conducted at Duke University and other top schools," she said. "I felt the evidence was strong that patients make remarkable progress when they know there are people pulling for them in a united way."

Robin suggested a prayer chain.

Jennifer said it couldn't hurt.

"I just kind of immediately clicked with her," Jennifer said. "She was a complete stranger who was eager to do something to help us—something that was meaningful and positive."

But Robin said she wouldn't proceed with the idea unless Jarrett approved.

Jennifer put Jarrett on the phone and Robin explained what she had in mind.

"Absolutely, I want it," Jarrett said, emphatically. "It's not my time to go."

And with that blessing, Robin hung up and began crafting the words to a prayer solely for a boy she had never met.

"I didn't want to set Jarrett up for unrealistic results," Jennifer said. "We were rational about his condition. But so many people would come up to me and say, 'We're concerned about Jarrett. What can we do to help?' I never knew what to say before. Now, I thought, I could hand them this prayer and ask them to join our chain."

Robin didn't pretend she could write words that would make Jarrett well.

"What I could do was stir up a lot of love around him," she said. "Everybody has this ability but not everyone is a writer. Therefore, my words make a lot of sense to those who don't know what to say to God."

Robin wrote a prayer that may seem too generic to some people. But that was on purpose. She wanted it to be distributed to Christians, Jews, Muslims and Buddhists. She asked that the readers adapt the wording to match their normal prayer practices.

"I wanted people to personalize it," she said. "Put it in Christ's name, if that's whom you say your prayers to." Robin, who is Jewish, didn't even know the Mynears were Roman Catholics. She didn't ask. It didn't matter.

"The more faiths, the better," Robin said. "God seems to like it when we put aside our differences."

The prayer was all positive. It didn't contain negative language such as "Please don't let Jarrett die." It was a thank you for sustaining him through the tough times:

Source of Life;
We have come together as one heart, one voice
To ask Your blessing on Jarrett Mynear.
Take our love and deliver it to him now.
Use it for his highest good.
May what we offer of ourselves comfort and soothe him.
Let his body receive the positive energy we offer,
Using it to strengthen the organs, muscles, bones, nerves and tissues that sustain life.
Be with him now, as You are with us, in life.
Bless Jarrett and his family with Your grace.
Thank you, thank You for the peace that embraces us in this effort.
May all be well.
May all be free.
Amen.

Jennifer e-mailed the prayer to all of her friends and relatives and asked them to pass it on. Robin did the same. The message requested that everyone say the prayer at 9 p.m., Eastern Standard Time, if possible. If not, to say it whenever it was convenient.

"Nine o'clock was about the time Jarrett was going to bed each night," Robin said. "I felt it would be good for him to slip into sleep while people were sending out thousands of beams of love."

The Internet can spread a message like wildlife. Consider how quickly a virus can infect computers around the world. And anyone who goes online knows how common it is to see the same jokes, chain letters and hoaxes pop up in their e-mail time and time again.

The prayer chain spread the same way. In a matter of days, Jennifer began to receive e-mail from all over North America, as well as Europe and the Middle East. Rosie O'Donnell posted the prayer on her website, after giving her third on-air update on Jarrett's condition.

"I got letters from missionaries in Africa who said they were saying the prayer," Jennifer said. "It was incredible to think each evening people all over the world were praying for him. Complete strangers would come up to me in stores and tell me they were saying the prayer.

"I was a little embarrassed at first. I thought people might think we were expecting too much. But even months later, I never had one negative comment about it."

=====

Much of Jarrett's faith was shaped by his friendship with Maurice Adkins, the man who fitted him with each artificial leg he had over the years.

Maurice owns a home in his native Pike County, three hours from Lexington. He goes back there to be with his wife every weekend. At least twice a year, they invite Jarrett for a visit.

Jarrett loves that mountain getaway, near hiking trails and fishing holes. Maurice would let Jarrett shoot a pistol at targets and he'd take him to go-cart tracks and knife shows.

"Jennifer told me I was going to turn her son into a redneck," Maurice laughed. "But the visits were good for both of us. It kept me young and kept him from thinking so much about his cancer."

Maurice was on a diving team in his youth and during one visit, when Jarrett was eight, the boy was determined to get his pal back on the board.

"I hadn't done a front flip in 25 years," Maurice remembered. "Jarrett wanted me to show him how it was done. I told him I was too old and out of shape but he wouldn't let me off the hook that easily."

"C'mon," Jarrett coaxed. "If you do one, I'll do one."

After much goading, Maurice stepped up on the diving board and looked out over the water in his backyard pool. He had a second thought.. then a third thought... and started to step back down. But then he spied Jarrett, sitting on the edge of the pool with catheters in his chest, wide-eyed with anticipation.

And in an instant, Maurice extended his arms in front of him and flipped into the pool, slicing the water like a hot knife through butter.

When he surfaced, Jarrett was standing there cheering.

Then the boy made his way to the diving board.

"He must've gone off that board ten times in a row," Maurice said. "I don't think he ever did completely flip over, but he swears he did."

What a sight it must've been–a grandfatherly figure and a tiny eight-year-old, both laughing and splashing like crazy in the pool, challenging each other to "do it again." And neither one of them had a right leg. Some might've questioned whether they had their right minds.

Maurice restores antique cars. His pride and joy is a cherry red 1934 Plymouth Coupe.

"It's really souped up," Maurice said.

Jarrett loves to go riding in the old car, sitting on a pillow so he can see over the dashboard and maybe so people in the other cars can see him when they pass.

Both driver and passenger feel pretty cool when they're "cruising."

"Once when I was taking him home, Jarrett said to me, 'I thought you said this was a hot rod. Why are you going so slow?'" Maurice said.

"So, I hit the pedal to the floor and the force pinned him back in the seat. His mother would've killed me if she had known.

"He straightened up and had a big smile on his face. He said, 'Do it again.' So, I did and we both laughed like hyenas. My wife stopped going out with us. She said we acted too silly and made too much noise. We embarrassed her!"

It was that spirit that inspired Maurice and, like Robin Silverman, he wanted to surround his friend with the positive power of prayer.

Maurice attends Shelby United Methodist Church, a country chapel he describes as "old-time Methodist."

He added Jarrett's name to the church's prayer list right after he met him as a toddler.

"The congregation prayed for him every week for years, even though it hadn't met him," Maurice said. "I kept telling the members how special he was and not a week went by when I didn't give them an update on his condition."

Finally, not long after the day of diving, Jarrett went to church with Maurice. He wanted to meet the people who had been praying for him and the congregation was happy to put a face with the name it had been lifting to the Lord.

The country preacher asked Jarrett if he'd like to say a few words–a question to which Jarrett never answered "no."

Jarrett walked to the front of the sanctuary and thanked the churchgoers for their support.

"I know you've been praying for me and that means a lot," Jarrett said. "Maurice told me that God put him and me together for a reason and it's been great. Maurice always puts me in a good mood. When I'm feeling down, I can call him and he makes me feel better. I think it's important to have good friends and he's been my best friend. And even though most of you don't know me, I know about you. You're all my friends too."

Jarrett's sincerity stirred the congregation.

"There wasn't a dry eye in the house," Maurice said. "The sermon was good that day but nothing was as uplifting as Jarrett's speech."

When the service was over, Maurice and Jarrett walked toward the car.

"Did you feel that?" Jarrett asked his host.

"Feel what?" Maurice asked back.

"God was in there," Jarrett said.

The observation caused Maurice to pause.

"Yes, He was Jarrett. And now He's out here. He's going with you wherever you go."

In 1999, Maurice developed complications related to a triple bypass years earlier. Tests right around Christmas showed an irregular heartbeat. Doctors told him there was a chance he wouldn't live much longer–news that sent Maurice into instant depression.

Jarrett didn't know how serious it was. Maurice hadn't wanted to worry him.

"The first night after coming home from the hospital, I felt sad and sorry for myself," Maurice recalled. "The phone rang at 10 o'clock that night, just as I was getting ready for bed. There was Jarrett's happy voice on the other end saying, 'Hey buddy, I thought you may need a little cheering up!'"

Maurice's mood changed on the spot.

"I thought, 'here's this kid who's been through so much and he's thinking about me.' I never asked God for another day after that. I realized how blessed I was. And it was Jarrett who opened my eyes."

In late 2000, as Jarrett struggled through his toughest time yet, the pair sat at a table in a pizza parlor, waiting for a pepperoni pie with extra cheese.

Maurice knew how bad things were. He had seen the blisters in Jarrett's throat and had heard from the boy's mother about the numerous tumors that had shown up on the most recent scans.

"You're not feeling too well, are you?" he asked Jarrett.

The boy reached his small hands across the table and took Maurice's hands. The tears began to flow.

"They think I'm gonna die," Jarrett confided.

"What do you think?"

"I don't think they're right," Jarrett said. "I can't go yet. I have too much to do."

"Then that's the way you handle it," Maurice instructed. "Keep doing all you need to do. God won't let you leave here with unfinished business."

"That's what I think too," Jarrett said. "I'm still perfecting my front flip."

41
Penny War

Just after Christmas, the principal at West Jessamine Middle School issued a challenge to the student body. He told the students if they could raise $3,000 to help pay for Jarrett's medical expenses, he would shave his head. And better still, the kids who raised the most money could do the shearing.

And the Penny War was on.

Several of the teachers had talked with Glen Teater, the principal, about doing something to help Jarrett's entire family. They really didn't need more toys for the cart at that time, but the bills had to be mounting. The teachers said the students seemed to be really down about the news that Jarrett was doing so poorly. Many of them had asked how they could "make it better."

"When the teachers came to me with the idea, I was reluctant at first," Jennifer said. "We were so much more fortunate than many of the families and we weren't comfortable having them collect money for our own benefit."

But the teachers and staff knew insurance didn't cover all of Jarrett's expenses. The Mynears spent more than $10,000 a year out of their own pockets. That had added up to more than $100,000 over the years. The school staff insisted a collection drive would be good for the students.

Doug and Jennifer gave their permission for the Penny War, on one condition. They'd put the money in the bank and let it draw interest. They'd use some for traveling expenses and medical bills, but they also wanted to find a way to make it benefit the school. Perhaps down the road, it would need library books or a computer or some other piece of equipment. Months later, the Mynears used some of the proceeds to fly Jarrett's friend Greg Siegman in from Chicago to conduct assemblies about diversity and racial harmony at several schools in the county.

The rules of a penny war are difficult to explain. The kids seemed to comprehend it better than the adults did.

Basically, a jar was placed in each homeroom and kids would

187

deposit their change there. A penny counted as one point. But the student could also go into other rooms and make deposits. Coins other than pennies resulted in negative points for that room. For example, if a jar had 25 pennies in it, that meant 25 points. But if a student dropped in a dime, ten points were subtracted. So, the jar would contain 35 cents, but be worth just 15 points.

It was a way to "slam" your competition while still causing the pot to grow. The competition grew fierce, with teachers also getting involved. Jars that one day looked completely copper-colored would show a top layer of silver the next day.

"Kids literally brought in buckets full of change," Jennifer said, laughing. "They were forcing their family members to cough it up."

Once again, it was an incredible show of school support and proof that giving can be as much fun as receiving.

At the end of January, Mr. Teater called an assembly to announce the result of "the war."

"Before I do this," he said, "I want us to welcome back our friend Jarrett Mynear."

Jarrett walked into the gym for the first time since mid-November. Every student rose and applauded. The cheers and whistles rang around the hollow room. Jennifer stood along a wall and wiped tears from her eyes.

Then Mr. Teater talked to the students about the sense of community that had developed over the past few weeks and reminded them again about what it means to be charitable.

The gym broke out into the school chant: "West is best... West is best.. West is best."

Mr. Teater let it continue for a couple of minutes, then quieted the crowd down with a wave of his arms.

"I guess you're wondering how much money we raised," he said. "Remember, I'm not going to shave my head unless it's $3,000."

The students fidgeted in the bleachers and smiled devilish grins. They were sure they had met the goal.

"Well, here's the total," Teater said, building suspense as he fumbled to unfold a sheet of paper.

"Let's see... it looks like... let me be sure... yeah... $6,500!"

The room burst out in laughter and applause. The take more than doubled the goal.

"Before I lose my hair, I want anybody in this room who had anything at all to do with this to stand and be recognized... even if you gave just one penny."

Everyone stood, including teachers, cooks, janitors and office aides.

Love isn't something you can hold in your hand, but it's something you can feel. Jarrett felt it multiplied 750 times as he looked at all those people on their feet. He later told his mom that assembly meant more to him than any award he'd ever received.

Two teachers brought a tarpaulin out to cover the gym floor and they turned a bucket upside down as a seat for Mr. Teater.

The five kids who had raised the most money were called up to help with the honors. Each one took a swipe with the electric clippers as the student body roared its approval and Mr. Teater's locks hit the floor.

Then they handed the clippers to Jarrett, who delighted in cutting a stripe from his principal's crown to his forehead.

Then, he stopped and reached into a bag at his side. Jarrett pulled out a child-sized wig.

"I thought you might want to wear this," Jarrett said, handing it to Mr. Teater. "I never really used it."

It was an ugly wig, Jennifer admits–one she had purchased years before, thinking Jarrett would be self-conscious about his baldness. That was an unfounded worry. The wig became more of a joke. It looked like a dead squirrel. Mr. Teater was welcome to it.

The principal was scheduled to go with the Kentucky delegation to Washington later that week. He would attend the inauguration of President George W. Bush.

"It will be cold in Washington," Jarrett said. "This wig will keep you warm."

Jennifer got a mental image of Mr. Teater meeting the president with the pathetic hairpiece balanced on top of his shiny pate. She laughed out loud.

A science teacher, Donny Loughry, took a straight razor and shaving cream and finished the job, leaving the principal with a sleek chrome dome.

Another teacher, whose hobby was sewing, came forward with two red and white fleece hats she had made. They had earflaps like

Elmer Fudd would wear. Jarrett and Mr. Teater both left the school that day sporting the funky headgear. To be truthful, Jarrett still felt miserable but the assembly had been a great morale booster.

As the buses pulled away, a custodian swept up the stray salt and pepper locks on the gym floor. The principal may've given up his hair, but everyone in the school had shown their roots–strands of compassion that were buried deep and would continue to grow.

By mid-March, the scans showed the tumors were shrinking. Jennifer was certain the Penny War and the prayer chain had made a difference.

Robin Silverman, the prayer chain's author, got to know Jarrett and his family better through the effort and she said the experience changed her life.

"Jarrett seems to know a secret about life that the rest of us just don't know," she said. "In his soul agreement, I believe he was told to come down here from Heaven and teach us all about love."

Jarrett shaves Principal Glen Teater's head, as curriculum coordinator Margie Maloney looks on. (Staff photo/Lexington Herald-Leader)

42
Reflection

As Jennifer stood in the warehouse on a warm spring day, facing boxes stacked to the ceiling, she thought about the big job she had ahead of her. She had an inventory list in one hand and a yellow highlighter in the other. She needed to see if everything ToysRUs.com shipped had actually made it to Lexington. This was the booty from a third appearance on The Rosie O'Donnell Show, in which the toy company had pledged to send another $10,000 worth of donations.

Jennifer would have to restack the boxes, putting toys for infants along one wall and separating those best suited for older boys and girls along another wall. It was incredible to see what the company had sent: building blocks, baby rattles, Barbie dolls, dress-up clothes for girls and cowboy hats for boys, Play-Doh molds, wood burning sets, model airplanes, Nerf basketballs and hoops, yo-yos, compact discs, music boxes, backpacks, plastic horses and rubber snakes. Soon, Terry Hagan of The Dream Factory would be there to help move boxes and warehouse workers would bring in pallets and forklifts to relocate the stacks away from the entrance.

But as she stood there waiting for the helping hands, in the musty space with sunlight streaming through skylights and cobwebs glistening in the rafters, it seemed as if she were facing a giant beast made of cardboard and packing tape.

"When The Joy Cart started, none of us had any idea what we were getting ourselves into," she said later. The pet project had turned into a monster, albeit a friendly one. When it needs to be fed, donors always come through. The cart never goes hungry.

There, in the warehouse in a lonely part of the city, is the part of The Joy Cart no one ever sees–the part that is hard work. In a back room, way beyond rows of business records and millions of documents that are kept there, is the toy storage room. It had once been a break room for employees of a large bakery that abandoned the warehouse nearly a decade ago

This isn't just a Toys R Us mountain. Other boxes contain toys collected by school groups, churches and civic clubs, and donations from stores that had cleared shelves as they went out of business. In some ways, the room is like a museum. Many of the toys are discontinued items–things you can't buy now. And every week, like clockwork, Jennifer goes there to pick and choose items to pack into the family van. The toys then go to the hospital to be loaded onto carts for the next run.

"It amazes me every time I go there to see how much people have donated," Jennifer said. "If I ever start to gripe about having so many boxes to climb over, I stop and remind myself that this is an outpouring of love from a lot of people who care about Jarrett and believe in his project."

The response had quite possibly given Jarrett the will to live during some tough times. It's what put the joy in The Joy Cart.

The warehouse is a good place to think.

Just six hours after Jarrett had been diagnosed with cancer for the first time, when he was two-and-a-half years old, a retired priest told Jennifer "to look for the good in this." It had made her angry.

"It's not what I wanted to hear," she said. "I wanted to throw him out of the hospital when he said that."

But now, when she wants to look for the good in Jarrett's situation, she can see it in this stuffy warehouse.

"We have been blessed because so many people have reached out to us," she said, "not only by giving toys, but also of their time. They've helped us clean the house, they've brought us meals, provided babysitting and prayed for us every night.

"We'd get bogged down thinking how we could pay everybody back and then just realized it would never be possible. When you can't pay back, you pay it forward and just do something nice for someone else."

That is the whole concept of The Joy Cart in a nutshell.

Jennifer thought about all the places they'd been, all the people they'd met, all the doors that had opened because of Jarrett's cancer.

Their son has lived a compressed life, doing more in his first twelve years than most people could hope to do in a lifetime.

"We really are better people because of what has happened," Jennifer said.

That doesn't mean she'd go back and do it all over again, given the chance to change things.

"It's absurd to think we're dancing in the streets saying cancer's been wonderful for us," she said. "No one would choose this."

Jarrett has been an inspiration to so many that Jennifer believes sometimes people think he is super-human.

"There were a couple of times when he had to unload his emotions. We learned early on not to waste too much energy dwelling on things we couldn't change. We didn't want him to spend time asking 'Why me?' and go on about how unfair it was. But we had to let him validate his feelings."

Only once did she really see Jarrett snap. It was in private at their home.

"He said, 'I'm sick of being little bitty, having to crane my neck every time I look at somebody. I'm sick of worrying about the port-o-cath in my side and at people expecting me to be happy all the time. And I wish the girls would look at me as someone they might want to go out with someday and not just as everybody's little buddy.'"

Jennifer let him vent.

"I thought, at least that once, it was healthy. It's normal to feel that way."

Jennifer knew how tough it was for her to suck it up and be tough sometimes. She couldn't imagine what it was like for a twelve-year-old boy.

"Sometimes, I'd be so tired I couldn't think straight," she said. "Many times I'd tell Doug to just get the car and drive us to a restaurant because I couldn't focus enough to put something on the stove. Jarrett's ability to keep it together always amazed me."

As she continued sifting through the donations, Jennifer thought how much better it was to be there than in the pediatric clinic, where she had spent a large portion of her life waiting for her son to go through his chemotherapy.

"It was just emotionally draining to sit there," she said. "Many of the children there are in the same condition as Jarrett or worse. It's a room full of parents watching their kids get infused with poisons. You're just immersed in the world of cancer.

"I've formed countless friendships with the other mothers who come there and I've watched many of them bury their children. I witnessed a six-year-old girl screaming at the top of her lungs, 'Just let me die!' That's why it's hard to accept it when well-meaning people say 'Look for the good in this.'"

She's also watched marriages break apart, as mothers had to quit their jobs.

"The wives say to their husbands, 'You don't know what it's like to spend all day at the clinic' and the husbands say, 'Well, you don't know it's like to be at work all day wondering what's happening but not being able to leave because someone has to bring home a paycheck.'"

She and Doug had held similar conversations.

But again, she looked at the donations stacked in front of her and thought how, despite all the work, Jarrett's idea had been their salvation. It gave him, and all of them, a reason to keep going.

"During the weeks when I couldn't run the cart and I left it in the hands of volunteers, I'd find myself wondering which kids had been at the hospital that week and how they were doing. And when Jarrett couldn't go, he'd ask me who was there. I'd see him get excited when he spied certain toys in the back of the van. He'd say 'so-and-so's there. He's gonna love that.'"

And even though she was too young to go on the patient floors at the children's hospital, Claire took ownership in The Joy Cart as well. She made suggestions about what toys to take to the little girls and always helped load the van.

"It was her way of being able to help out," Jennifer said.

As she got older, Jarrett worried that Claire might be jealous of all the attention he received. But, somewhat surprisingly, her parents marveled at the way she handled Jarrett's fame.

She refused to be overlooked. For one thing, she was bigger than Jarrett. At age nine, her 4'10" height was nearly a foot taller than her brother's twelve-year-old frame. She weighed 30 pounds more.

"When a stranger ignored her, it probably wasn't on purpose," Jennifer said. "They probably didn't even know Jarrett had a little sister."

Time and time again, Doug and Jennifer watched Claire go up and introduce herself to someone who was talking to Jarrett.

"She'd stick out her hand and proudly say, 'I'm Claire. I'm his sister and I gave him my bone marrow.'"

It always made them smile.

When Jarrett had speeches and other public appearances, Claire often stayed home, simply because she didn't want to go.

"She had had more than her fill of banquets and boring speeches," Jennifer said. "We didn't want people to think we were leaving her behind. For her, it was a treat to get a night at home with her own babysitter. Then she was the center of attention in her own domain."

Children with ADHD need as much predictability as possible and with the Mynears' situation, nothing was predictable.

"When Claire first went to school, she couldn't handle it if someone else came to pick her up after school, even someone she knew and loved," Jennifer said. "If I wasn't there, she'd immediately worry that something was wrong with Jarrett."

That's why Jennifer made it a point to be in the school's parking lot each day, as often as possible, even when it meant a half-hour drive from the hospital, to home and back to the hospital.

"But the longer she was in school and socializing with other people, the more she matured," Jennifer said. "Now, she's better able to handle a lack of predictability."

The patients at the hospital also had trouble dealing with a break from the routine. One week, about three months after The Joy Cart began, there was just no one available to take it on its regular Tuesday night run–the only time that's ever happened.

A young cancer patient named Stanley stayed awake until 2 a.m. He just knew Jarrett would be coming. The boy's mother told him Jarrett is not like Santa Claus. He doesn't come in the middle of the night. But Stanley insisted that Jarrett wouldn't forget him.

Finally, the nurses found an unopened toy they had stashed away in the playroom and gave it to him, telling him it was from Jarrett.

Stanley fell asleep, clutching a Matchbox car in his hand.

Jennifer remembered the story and laughed out loud.

That was the good in all this.

43
Sequel

Melinda Morrison knew a lot of business and media leaders in Seattle and the more she thought about it, the more she knew it was the right place for Jarrett's Joy Cart II. He had spent so much time in the city; it was where he had his stem cell transplants and there was a lot about the northwest that Jarrett loved.

So right after the segment aired on Oprah, she began working behind the scenes in a much more proactive way than the Mynears knew.

Melinda showed the videotape and several press clippings to the administrators at the Seattle Children's Hospital. They liked the idea.

That hospital had recently teamed with "The Hutch." Children who came from all over the world for bone marrow and stem cell transplants stayed there. It had more than 600 beds–twelve times more than the children's hospital in Kentucky.

Melinda contacted other people the Mynears knew there, including Jarrett's former teacher, Susan Sever, and Paul Gordon, the young documentary producer he had met at the Prudential Spirit of Community awards. They promised to help.

And she called on Howard Lincoln, the CEO of the Seattle Mariners. He told Melinda whenever she was ready, the organization would set up a royal welcome for Jarrett by providing his family with a hotel room and hosting a reception for them at the ballpark.

Melinda took a leave of absence from the Oprah show.

"I e-mailed her (Oprah) and told her I was following the advice she always preaches–that you should follow your passion," Melinda said.

She worked feverishly to collect toys and line up sponsors and when she had everything in order, Melinda called Jennifer.

"I need you to be in Seattle the first week in April," she said over the phone, wanting Jarrett to be at the Mariner's season opener.

"Well, I'm not sure we can make it," Jennifer said. "Everything is touch and go with Jarrett right now. He may not be able to travel."

But Melinda made Jennifer promise to try to make the trip if at all possible. She understood about the uncertainty of Jarrett's health. All she was asking was that she and Doug clear their work schedules and be on standby, in the event Jarrett was having a good week.

"I bought the plane tickets," Melinda said. "I just put them on my credit card. I didn't care. I'd figure out how to pay for them later."

When his parents told Jarrett about the planned rollout of a second Joy Cart in Seattle, he perked up. It was what he had hoped for.

"I didn't do this to become famous," he said. "But I would like to see it expand beyond Kentucky. I want to be there for the ribbon cutting."

The family had plane tickets for Saturday, March 31st. But the night before, Jarrett came down with a fever. A quick trip to the doctor resulted in a night in the hospital. Based on past experience, the family wasn't about to fly while Jarrett was running a temperature.

But by Monday, Jarrett seemed as spunky as ever. His parents knew he was eager to go to Seattle. And, even though they seldom allowed themselves to think that way, they realized his days may be numbered.

"We wanted him to see his good works being multiplied," Jennifer said. "He had been so sick and so weak since November, we thought we'd better take this window of opportunity. This may be the best he'd ever feel again."

Jennifer called Melinda and told her they'd come, because she had a strong feeling this would be the family's last vacation as a foursome.

That thought broke Melinda's heart.

So, Doug, Jennifer, Claire and Jarrett flew to Seattle April 2nd. Melinda met them at the airport.

"I wasn't prepared to see Jarrett that way," she said. "He was really weak and his dad carried him. I didn't know if I could handle it."

The family rented a car and headed to the Westin Hotel, where they were guests of the Mariners.

When they opened the door to their room, it was the most beautiful suite they had ever stayed in. It had two bedrooms with separate space for the kids. It was clear the Mariners didn't do anything halfway.

The next afternoon, the family went to SAFECO Field and got the grand tour.

During the practice session, almost every player came over to shake Jarrett's hand and pose for pictures with him. It was clear they had been briefed about their special guest and what he had accomplished.

"Jarrett rallied," Melinda observed. "He seemed so much stronger than he had the day before. He was running on adrenaline and sheer willpower."

Jarrett asked infielder Mark McLemore if he'd sign a baseball. McLemore pulled a ball out of his own pocket and said, "You don't need my autograph, I need yours. I saw you on Oprah."

"They were all the nicest bunch of guys," Jennifer said. "It was incredible. They went out on the field to do stretches and they made sure Jarrett did them, too."

When the players left the field to go to the dressing rooms, they invited Doug and Jarrett in. The pair just hung out in the clubhouse a while, taking in all of the pre-game atmosphere.

The family had dinner in the president's suite, enjoying the all-they-could eat buffet. It sure beat stadium hot dogs.

About fifteen minutes before the team was about to meet the Oakland Athletics on that cold night, a Mariners staffer escorted the family back down to the edge of the field. The public address system blared as the announcer told the crowd about that night's ceremonial first pitch.

Jarrett's name flashed on the scoreboard in huge white lights and the fans in the stands watched a short video clip that explained The Joy Cart. Melinda had supplied some of her video from the Oprah show. The Mariners production department had also dropped in some last-minute scenes from Jarrett's pre-game visits with the players.

"Chills ran up my spine as I looked up at that scoreboard and all those people," Jennifer said. "Here we were two thousand miles from home and our son was the center of attention. To see all of his work coming to fruition in another city was almost unbelievable."

Melinda also felt the electricity. Even months later, she couldn't talk about it without crying.

"It was the highlight of my life so far," she said.

When the clip ended, the Mariner's mascot–a large costumed

moose–led Jarrett to a spot just in front of the pitcher's mound.

Forty-five thousand fans stood and cheered.

"I thought, 'OK, I've done what I wanted to do, I can't cure him but this is the best I can do,'" Melinda said.

Jarrett wound up and let the ball fly right across home plate. The crowd responded with applause that echoed through the chilly night air.

The moose presented Jarrett with two large shopping bags full of Mariners souvenirs–T-shirts, caps, teddy bears and pennants that he could use to help stock the newest Joy Cart.

A member of the team's organization walked the family back to the owner's suite where they spent the evening with Melinda and several other people who made the night possible, including owner Howard Lincoln and executives from Boeing.

Although renowned athletes and executives filled the stadium, Jarrett seemed to be the biggest man there.

Melinda relished watching Jarrett as he enjoyed every minute of the evening.

"He was chatting with the bartender and the servers in the presidential suite as if to say 'this is the way I'm supposed to be treated,'" she said, laughing.

As the evening wore on, Jennifer decided it was time to go. Another big day was ahead, but it was just the seventh inning. It was the only time Melinda had seen Jarrett get testy.

"I'm not ready to go," Jarrett protested.

"Ready or not, it's time," Jennifer responded.

"I get an allowance. You go on. I'll use my own money to get a taxi," Jarrett said.

"No, you'll go with us now," Jennifer insisted.

"Mom, I know what I can handle better than you. Let me stay," he replied, trying to play the sympathy card.

But his mother won the battle.

Melinda knew she probably shouldn't delight in witnessing the argument. But it was the payoff to all of her planning. It meant Jarrett was having a great time.

The next day, with the excitement of the game not yet worn off, Jarrett and his family went to the Seattle Children's Hospital.

They walked into the playroom and the scene took them back two years. It was much like the news conference in Kentucky in 1999 when they had the inaugural run of Jarrett's Joy Cart. Just like then, reporters, television cameras and still photographers filled the room. Hospital administrators, doctors and nurses lined the walls.

One of the first people Doug and Jennifer noticed was John Hayes, the volunteer from The Hutch who had arranged the troll skit and so many other surprises for Jarrett. It had been five years since they'd seen each other. Walt Disney was right. It's a small world after all.

"I thought it was great for all these people he had known to see he had done this amazing thing," Melinda said.

Once again, Jarrett's parents stood back and watched in wonder as their son talked to the media about the idea behind The Joy Cart–the simple yet profound message he had repeated so many times.

"This is about giving kids something to look forward to," Jarrett said again, with as much conviction as the first time he uttered the phrase.

A hospital cart sat in front of the room, loaded with stuffed animals, puzzles, books and trinkets. The sign on the front of it said **"JARRETT'S SEATTLE JOY CART."** A red ribbon draped across the front.

Melinda handed Jarrett a pair of scissors and he bent down on his artificial right knee and snipped the ribbon in two.

Cameras flashed and two pre-selected children came in for the photo op, picking the first two toys off the cart.

They turned and smiled.

The joy had spread.

Jarrett autographs a baseball for Mark McLemore of
the Seattle Mariners. (Photo by Gerry Morrison)

Afterword

Jarrett beat the odds so many times that there was nothing predictable about him. He was proof that a positive attitude could be better than any medicine.

"He really does care about other people and he's found the perfect way to communicate that," Dr. Moscow said when he knew the end was near. "He has found the perfect way to harness his natural interest in other patients."

"So many people care very deeply about him," the doctor said. "Eventually, we'll run out of tricks. We'll reach into our bag and there will be nothing left. Jarrett knows that. That's why it's so important that he makes every day of his life special."

In the final months, there were still special days. A highlight for Jarrett was the opportunity to carry the Olympic torch for two blocks on a Lexington street as the relay made its way to the winter games in Salt Lake City. Cheerleaders, classmates, family and friends rooted him on, not knowing he had lost most of the feeling in his right arm.

In June 2002, he was well enough to join his aunt, Margaret Wagner, as she began making the rounds with a third Joy Cart, this time at Kosair Children's Hospital in Louisville.

The bag came up empty Oct. 4, 2002. Jarrett died at the UK Children's Hospital after weeks of struggle as his body grew weaker and the tumors grew larger. The doctors literally ran out of options as the boy's liver and kidneys shut down.

At the funeral four days later, the Rev. Linh Nguyen reminded 600 mourners that Jarrett would want them to be happy for him.

"He was a Wonder Boy who taught us to love as a kid loves," the priest said, noting that Jarrett wasn't impressed by power or prestige and that he didn't notice race, religion or gender.

"He had a passion to take away the pain of other children," Nguyen eulogized. "He wanted us to remember that it's with a simple toy that children sit together and play. There we find Christ; there we find common peace and love."

Midway through the funeral, the priest strayed from his prepared script, pausing to tell the congregation that Jarrett was a great kid

203

because he had great parents. Looking at Doug and Jennifer, he said, "You are what made him what he was."

The congregation rose in unison to give the Mynears a standing ovation.

The sermon ended with a moment that Jarrett would've loved. Father Linh lifted a giant water gun above Jarrett's casket, pumped the handle, and sprayed the crowd. Laughter rang through the church. That was the right way to remember a boy who never wanted anyone to shed tears for him.

When the funeral procession entered the gates of Lexington Cemetery, six police officers stood at attention – two SWAT members, two officers mounted on horses, a patrolman from the bicycle unit and an officer with a dog from the canine patrol. The police loved Jarrett and wanted to treat him as a fallen officer. At the gravesite, the boy received a 15-gun salute.

The Joy Cart still rolls every Tuesday evening in Lexington, every Wednesday afternoon in Seattle, and each Thursday in Louisville. The family has been contacted by people who want to start carts in Vancouver, Washington; Portland, Oregon; and Chicago. There's no way to know how many similar projects have been started or are in the works. E-mail suggests the number could be in the hundreds. Jarrett's story has been an inspiration to thousands of people who have looked for ways to commit random acts of kindness.

I saw Jarrett in the hospital just a couple of hours before he died. I'd like to think he was aware that I came by. There's no way to really know what he comprehended.

I picture him now in Heaven, standing tall with a full head of wavy hair and two strong legs. He's out of pain and no doubt running around with all of the energy he built up and never got to use here on Earth. If God has a dog, Jarrett probably takes it for a walk every morning.

Jarrett's family asked me to sign a copy of this book to be buried with him. I felt honored and wrote simply:

Jarrett,
The best chapters of your story are yet to come. Take good notes and we'll talk about it the next time we meet.
Your friend,
Marvin

Jarrett passes off the Olympic Torch as it travels through Lexington on its way to Salt Lake City, December 17, 2001.

Links

To keep up to date with Jarrett's accomplishments, visit *www.thejoycart.com*.

Additional information about the agencies mentioned in this book can be found through the following links:

Jarrett's Seattle Joy Cart: Seattle Children's Hospital, 4800 Sand Point Way NE, P.O. Box 5371, Seattle, WA 98105. (206) 526-2000. *www.seattlechildrens.org*

The Dream Factory: 1-800-456-7556. *www.dreamfactoryinc.org*

Indian Summer Camp: Friends of Indian Summer, P.O. Box 24337, Louisville, KY 40224. (502) 491-8518. *www.iscamp.org*

Children's Oncology Camp Association: 1-800-737-2667. *www.coca-intl.org*

University of Kentucky Children's Hospital: 800 Rose Street, Lexington, KY 40508. (859) 323-6000. *www.mc.uky.edu/chuk*

Prudential Spirit of Community Awards:
www.prudential.com/community/spirit

American Institute for Public Service: 100 W. 10th Street, Suite 215, Wilmington, DE 19801. (302) 622-9101. *www.aips.org*

National Marrow Donor Program: 300 Broadway Street NE, Suite 500, Minneapolis, MN 55413. 1-800-MARROW2. *www.marrow.org*

Patient Advocate Foundation: 753 Thimble Shoals Blvd., Suite B, Newport News, VA 23606. 1-800-532-5274. *www.patientadvocate.org*

11-10-02 Foundation: *www.brunchbunch.com*

Printed in the United States
43640LVS00002B/295

9 781588 511447